THE Best IS YET Ahead

PRESSING TOWARD PROPHETIC FULFILLMENT

Chuck D. Pierce
and
Rebecca Wagner Sytsema

WAGNER
PUBLICATIONS

The Best is Yet Ahead
Copyright © 2001
by Chuck D. Pierce and Rebecca Wagner Sytsema
ISBN 1-58502-023-0

Published by
Wagner Publications
11005 N. Highway 83
Colorado Springs, CO 80921
www.wagnerpublications.org

Cover design by
Imagestudios
100 East St. Suite 105
Colorado Springs, CO 80903
719-578-0351

Edited by
C. Lil Walker

Interior design by
Rebecca Sytsema

Rights for publishing this book in other languages are contracted by Gospel Literature International (GLINT). GLINT also provides technical help for the adaptation, translation, and publishing of Bible study resources and books in scores of languages worldwide. For further information, contact GLINT, P.O. Box 4060, Ontario, CA 91761-1003, USA. You may also send e-mail to glintint@aol.com, or visit their web site at www.glint.org.

2 3 4 5 6 7 8 9   07 06 05 04 03 02

Dedication

This book is lovingly dedicated to our children:

Daniel Pierce
Rebekah Pierce
John Mark Pierce
Joseph Pierce
Isaac Pierce
Ethan Pierce
Nicholas Sytsema
Samuel Sytsema
All of our children yet to come

and

To all of our children's children.

Dear ones, do not fear, for *the best is yet ahead!*

Contents

When God knit you together in your mother's womb, He had a distinct purpose and timing for your life. He knew before the foundation of the world the time frame for your birth. At that point of conception, your life cycle began.

During our life cycle, we have many choices. Each day when we arise, our first thought should be, "Choose you this day whom you will serve." If we serve God we will succeed in the redemptive plan for which He created us. We will be aware of His presence. We will know when we deviate from His ultimate plan. We will also know when the enemy of our soul, Satan, attempts to interrupt that life cycle of God.

The Creator of the universe has created you and has an incredible plan for your life. Choose today whom you will serve so that your future is assured. Know this: *the best is yet ahead!*

A dear friend, Don MacAlpine, recently wrote this wonderful testimony:

Pilot Ejection of 1st Lt. Don MacAlpine
Mona Loa, Hawaii

It was the day before Thanksgiving, 1955, and I was the wingman of a two plane section. We were flying FJ-2's on a training mission and had decided to go to the big island of Hawaii and buzz the inside of Mona Loa, a volcanic crater.

As we were descending, I felt and heard an explosion from the aft end of my aircraft. I radioed my section leader and advised him. I then put out a May Day call and told them where I was and what had happened. About this time one of two red warning lights came on. (One warning light means that there is a fire in the aft end and nothing will happen until your cables burn through. The other warning light means you have approximately 4 seconds until the plane blows.) I couldn't tell which light was on – the whole cabin lit up red. I pulled the ejection bar and thought I had radioed my section leader that I was going out. He never heard it.

Once clear of my plane, I pulled my rip cord which came out so easily that I thought it didn't work. My parachute then opened and I thought: "All is well." My plane then crashed into the 1859 Lava Flow. Due to a full load of fuel aboard and the resulting explosion, there wasn't much left of the plane.

The whole mountainside was lava and I landed on a flat rock. The chute snagged on a small mesquite bush. My section leader was circling overhead and I wanted to advise him that I was okay. It seemed like forever for me to stand up, retrieve a flare and set it off, but he had only circled for a quarter of a circle. I knew we were too high for a helicopter rescue, so I walked back to the crash site and spent a cold, wet night waiting for the rescue squad to arrive.

The following day the rescue squad arrived, and checked the accident scene. Afterwards, I realized that I had a guardian angel looking after me. The lava rock was so sharp that the entire rescue team had to turn in their boots for new ones. Also, that small mesquite bush was the only one in about five square miles. The wind was of a high enough velocity to have dragged me over the rocks. The sharpness of these rocks would certainly have killed me. However, that one lone bush snagged me, and prevented me from being cut into shreds. Praise God!!! The bush became the manifestation of God in my life. Just as Moses experienced God in a bush, so did I.

At that point, even though I was not closely related to the Lord, I knew He had a plan for my life. I had seen Him in the bush. From that day forward, I have sought to follow after that plan so that my destiny could be fulfilled.

Just as Abraham found His provision for the future of his generations in a bush, and just as Moses found his call (which resulted in the destiny of a nation) in a bush, so Don also met God supernaturally in a bush. Our prayer for you as your read this book is that you will be able to open your eyes and see God in the circumstances and situations around you. He is Jehovah Jireh, the One who will see to it that your destiny has been provided for and is made complete.

Blessings,
Chuck D. Pierce
Rebecca Wagner Sytsema

CHAPTER ONE

God's *Now* Time
for Your Life!

For I know the thoughts that I think toward you, says the LORD,
thoughts of peace and not of evil,
to give you a future and a hope (Jer. 29:11).

H ave you ever gotten so caught in a hard place that you won-
dered if you could escape? Have you ever waited so long for
a promise to manifest that you lost hope? Have you known that
God has given you a promise that has yet to be fulfilled? One
morning I ("I" in this book refers to Chuck) awoke with the following words ringing through my spirit, "*The best is yet ahead. Do not
be discouraged by what you see for I can fulfill that which I have
for your life.*" I knew it was God.

The Truth About the Future

Is the best yet ahead? The truth is that for the believer in Christ, the
best is always ahead! We have a wonderful promise for our fu-

ture—an eternal promise of communion with God. The Bible clearly tells us that we don't live down here on earth with our sights set only on what is temporal, but that we are to have a view of eternity and operate from that perspective. God will give us grace to endure what is going on in our temporal world until we come into the fullness of our eternal destiny, which is with Him. This really is the bottom line. Even in our greatest hour here on earth, our best is still ahead.

But is that all there is? Is our only hope for prophetic fulfillment in eternity? What about our destiny while we are still here on earth? Yes, there is destiny to fulfill. Yes, there is more than grace to just endure our circumstances until the Lord calls us to Himself. And yes, God does have a wonderful plan for our temporal existence that will flow into our eternal communion with Him.

A Time of Birth

November 3, 1984 was a day of prophetic fulfillment for the Pierce family. It was on that autumn day in Tomball, Texas that our beautiful daughter, Rebekah, was born. What a joyful day it was—one that followed years of anguish and waiting, believing that God would come through on His word. It was a day of prophetic fulfillment because in 1980 God spoke to my wife, Pam, and assured her that she would have twins. At that time, however, she was barren. What an incredible promise to a woman who can't even conceive!

Pam's womb was filled with endometriosis—a disease that kept her body hostile to conception. The eggs were in her, but they were never able to connect in a way that would sustain life. In other words, the potential was there, but something was blocking it from forming and being nurtured so that life could result. There is much potential in many of us to conceive and bring God's plan to fullness for our life. However, there are many issues that keep us from seeing a fulfillment of God's purpose. These are the issues that we want to address in this book.

Pam knew that for God to give her twins, He would have to heal her. She had already been waiting for six years to conceive, and would wait for four more before her healing came. But after ten years, God kept His word and His prophetic promise to her was fulfilled.

There were many things that God had to set in order or rearrange before we saw the fruition of His promise. One of those things was our home. Before we had children our home was a beautiful show place. We could always find a comfortable chair to sit in and enjoy the quiet and the order. But, perfect as it was, our home was sterile.

For us to have children, we had to be willing to let go of our lifestyle. We had to be willing to have our perfect home messed up. We had to be willing to deal with spit-up on our carpet and the smell of dirty diapers in the air. We had to be ready for bloody noses, muddy shoes, noisy music, and to have dogs, cats, birds, and even snakes roaming through our home. We had to be ready for bickering and fights, for endless appointments, and for boyfriends and girlfriends. To come out of a place of barrenness and sterility, we had to be ready to receive the physical manifestation and all that that would represent in our lives, including obeying the Lord every step of the way.

Let the Healing Begin

There is a perfect time for each of us in our lives when we need to move forward into God's destiny and ultimate plan. I believe most of us want to have God's plan for our lives, but **we** must make the choice to do what He asks us to do. In our lives, there was a series of steps that Pam and I had to go through in order to see our promise of children fulfilled:

1. I had to obey the Lord and encourage Pam to quit her secular job.
2. The Lord brought a wonderful child into our life which we adopted as an infant.
3. The Lord required me to leave my secular job and go fulltime into ministry.
4. The Lord required us both to take positions at one of the largest children's homes in East Texas.
5. God began to extend to me my missions call by focusing me on the Soviet Union.
6. God had us deal with any sin, both personally and generationally, that could hinder us from receiving our promise.
7. God had Pam go to our pastor and have him pray for her.
8. The Spirit of the Lord began to teach us the principle of following after God. He spoke two words to us: *Follow Me.*
9. The Spirit of God visited me with revelation for the former Soviet Union and asked me to deliver that revelation to a key mission leader.
10. God also asked us to go to a conference that was contrary to the church we were attending at the time.
11. God asked my wife to raise her hands to worship in a way she had never worshiped before.
12. He asked us to respond to His Spirit, as His Spirit and power began to fall on us both at that conference.

As a result of these steps of obedience, culminating at the conference when Pam, against her nature, raised her hands in worship to God, she was healed instantly by the power of God invading her body and actually knocking the clots out that were in her uterus. I say *instantly,* but all the steps of obedience listed above took years of discipline. After that conference, however, Pam started her first normal menstrual cycle, and as a result her womb was no longer hostile. She conceived within two weeks. Not only did she conceive then, but she conceived four more times.

Obviously, these are not the same steps of obedience the Lord has for everyone, but there are steps of obedience that can lead anyone to prophetic fulfillment. Out of our willingness to allow the Lord to mess up our home and disrupt our lives, He eventually gave us beautiful, wonderful children. Where there were once many places to sit and enjoy the quiet, today you can hardly find a seat in the Pierce home. But it is a home filled with love, life, and promise for the future. Despite all the noise and all the commotion, we would never willingly go back to that place of sterility where our promises were locked up within us.

Prophetic fulfillment is often a messy process that can seem to interrupt the order of life. Yet even in the midst of drastic changes, there is a great joy in knowing that we are moving toward God's destiny. Our prayer for you as you read this book is that you will experience the joy of prophetic fulfillment in your own life.

Standing on the Promises

God has a future and a hope for everyone reading this book! He has given us promises for salvation, inheritance, and spiritual life. A promise is like a promissory note on which we can base our future. God has every intention of fulfilling His promises to us. This is a statement that we can take to the bank! This is a sure foundation upon which we can confidently stand.

But how do we know God's plan for our lives? The only way is through a covenant relationship with Him. From our covenant relationship, we discover God's plan for our destiny. God has many ways of revealing to us His desire for our lives. We may get an "I-know-

that-I-know" feeling within our hearts. We may encounter circumstances that we know have been directed by God that will open or
close doors. We may have an urging or intense desire that God is
stirring within us—something we know we need to do in our life.
We may have supernatural encounters such as dreams, visions, or
miracles. We may be reading the Bible and see a pattern that illumi-
nates to us that is very appropriate for our life. Or, we may have a
glimpse of God's destiny for us through prophetic words we receive.

No matter what our experience has been, we all have promises
from God giving us a future and a hope. He has a plan and a destiny
for each of us, and He is working all things together for good to
position us properly so His plans can be fulfilled. Each time we
respond to Him in obedience, we see progress in the overall fulfillment of our earthly purpose. This process and progression is what
we call *prophetic fulfillment.*

God's *Now* Time

There are seasons in our lives that are *now* times—times of prophetic fulfillment when God's promises are being manifested. In
the natural cycle of life there are seasons. Some seasons are filled
with desolation; but in those times we can take comfort in knowing
that every season has a timeframe. There is a time when desolation
ends and prophetic fulfillment begins. In his tremendous book, *God's
Timing for Your Life*, Dutch Sheets says, "Life is a series of changes—
a process of going from the old to the new—from *chronos* [a general
process of time] to *kairos* [an opportune, strategic, or *now* time].
Growth, change, revival—all are processes. Life is connected. Not
understanding this, we tend to despise the *chronos* times of preparing, sowing, believing and persevering.... We're not losing or
wasting time, we're investing it. And if we do so faithfully, the shift
will come."[1]

That was the case in our family when ten years of barrenness came to an end with the birth of our first child. When a time of desolation or wilderness ends and a new season of promise begins; those are God's *now* times.

In Daniel 9, we see a biblical example of a desolation season coming to an end so that a season of prophetic fulfillment could begin. Israel had been in captivity in Babylon for 70 years and was still in bondage when Daniel began reading the prophecies of Jeremiah: "…in the first year of his reign I, Daniel, understood by the books the number of the years specified by the word of the LORD through Jeremiah the prophet, that He would accomplish seventy years in the desolations of Jerusalem" (v.2). As he read, Daniel suddenly understood that there was a prophecy given many years before, and *now* was the time for the prophecy to be fulfilled. The 70 years of desolation that Jeremiah had prophesied had been completed and the time had come to break out of captivity.

God always has *now* times in our lives. Daniel knew it was time for this word to be fulfilled and for captivity to end. We, like Daniel, also need to come to a place where we understand God's time sequence. In my own life I know that when it is time for a desolation season to end, I want it done and its effects off of me. And once I get out of it, I don't want to turn back. That's the attitude we need to have in moving forward into prophetic fulfillment. We need to be in close enough relationship to God so that we know when to start into a new sequence and a new cycle of life. We need to know when it is time to cast off our desolation and move into a new season.

Breaking Out of Desolation

"Then I set my face toward the Lord God to make request by prayer and supplications, with fasting, sackcloth, and ashes" (v.3). As

Daniel came to an understanding that the times were changing and that Israel needed to break out of captivity, he did two things: He turned to God and dialoged with Him through prayer and supplications. Next, he began to deny himself through fasting so that all desolation could be broken. By doing these two things, he reconciled himself with God and, as a representative of Israel, broke out of the past season of desolation. This allowed the process to begin for them to break out of captivity and move into their future.

God is breaking desolation off His promises to us, personally, corporately, and territorially, and hell hates it. Any time we are getting ready to break forth into a new season of prophetic fulfillment, Satan will oppose us to keep us in the desolation of the past. There is a three-step process for us to be aware of as we move out of desolation toward *now* times in our lives:

1. God gives an intercessory call.

As was the case with Daniel, the first thing God often does is to release an intercessory burden in our lives. A burden is a deep impression of God's heart and will within our spirit. This burden feels like a weight or a stirring within us that is so strong that we must respond to God so change can come into our lives or environment. This is how intercession begins.

Intercession always proceeds what God is doing to break desolation from our lives. Prophetic fulfillment is a continuing process. In other words, all that God has done, even in the midst of the desolation season, has a purpose and will work together to move us into what He has for us in our new place. Dutch Sheets writes, "God wants to shift our thinking from becoming discouraged during these times to realizing the necessity of *chronos* seasons.... Knowing that we are cooperating with God and giving Him what He needs to bring the new, we can rejoice over, rather than despise, small beginnings."[2]

We need to get in line with what God has been doing and connect ourselves with it for our *now* season. Consequently, we need to respond to the prompting of the Holy Spirit to align ourself with God's mind and connect with His heart so we can move forward. This can only happen by communicating with a holy, sovereign God. As we come into agreement with God through His intercessory call to us, He will propel us out of the desolate circumstances that are abounding around us and into prophetic fulfillment.

In Ezekiel 22, God was ready to restore the people of Judah. In verses 23-29, God describes how the priests had

Prophetic fulfillment is a continuing process. In other words, all that God has done, even in the midst of the desolation season, has a purpose and will work together to move us into what He has for us in our new place.

been unholy, the prophets had been conspirators, the government officials had been like ravenous wolves, and the people had fallen into divination. Nevertheless, in verse 30, God says that if He can find one person who will make a wall and stand in the gap before Him on behalf of the land, He would then reverse everything the prophets, priests, and government officials had done wrong. He even promised to reverse the sinful corruption into which the people had fallen. He would do all of this if He could just find someone to meet with Him.

Intercession is defined as reaching or meeting someone to pressure them strongly to change a situation. Hebrews 7:25 says of

Jesus, "Therefore He is also able to save to the uttermost those who come to God through Him, since He always lives to make intercession for them." Christ is available to us to make intercession for us. That is what an intercessory call is about. The Spirit of God will co-labor with us and reveal to us our plan of escape and way out of desolation. But we must be willing to pray. We must be willing to meet with God until we gain strategy for moving forward, and then take a stand against the enemy who would seek to keep us bound in desolation. If we will do that, God will not only break us out of our desolation, but He will bring us out of whatever corruption we may have fallen into in our place of desolation. He will cleanse, renew, and restore us to a place of communion with Him.

2. God revives unfulfilled prophetic destiny.

As we come into agreement with God through intercession, God often reminds us of His plan of prophetic destiny, as Daniel discovered. Daniel had to go back 70 years to find out what God had promised the people of Israel. The prophet Jeremiah had prophesied in Jeremiah 25 that the whole land would go into desolation and would serve the King of Babylon for 70 years (v. 11). As Daniel received the prayer burden from God, he was able to understand this word that Jeremiah the prophet had spoken. It was now time for the power of desolation to be broken, and for restoration to begin!

That's how it is with us many times. Some of our grandparents and great grandparents had incredible prophetic destiny that never got completed. We need to understand how their prophetic inheritance became captive to the enemy. We also need to understand how the generational blessings of God have not been fulfilled.

I had to come to an understanding of unfulfilled prophetic destiny in my own life through watching my father. My father was a man who had a great deal of potential. However, he made bad choices. The path he chose for himself had corruption and defilement. Instead of glorifying God, his path ended with him dying a premature death. His destiny was never fulfilled.

God has created each one of us to reflect His glory. When we understand our identity in Him and begin to come into the fullness of that identity, His glory is seen through us. The absence of His glory indicates a curse. A curse working in our life brings desolation and postponement to the fulfillment of His promises. By seeing the mess that my father had made of his own life and even by being abused by his hand, I could have said, "O woe is me, look at what my father did." Instead I found myself saying, "Look at what my father could have been. Look what he could have accomplished had he allowed God to bring him into His ultimate plan for his life. Look at what should have been that wasn't."

The Lord even met me once and revealed the overwhelming love that He had for my earthly father. When I saw how much love God had for him, and what an incredible plan God had for him, I immediately said, "Lord, let me come into the fullness of not only my life, but accomplish the things that were meant in his generation that were sent astray by his alignment with the enemy."

I have learned, as we will discuss further in Chapter Five, that prophetic destiny is often tied in with our generations. Therefore, I want to be sure that I somehow complete what God has intended for my bloodline. I need to become successful where there has been failure in my family. I need to overcome the enemy where others in my bloodline did not withstand him. To have prophetic fulfillment in our own lives, we need to allow the Lord to revive the unfulfilled prophetic destiny in our family line, and give us a success mentality of completion and fulfillment.

3. God calls us to prophesy into our destiny.

As hard as it is for many to believe, God has chosen to use us as a necessary link to bring His will to earth. He calls us to come into dialog with Him, listen to His voice, and gain prophetic revelation so the hope of our calling can be fulfilled. He asks us to take that revelation and prophesy it into the earth realm.

This action of declaring prophetic revelation is called prophetic intercession. Barbara Wentroble says, "Prophetic intercession is one type of prayer that unlocks miracles and releases the blessings of God.... The Body of Christ stands today in the womb of the dawn of a new day (see Ps. 110:3). We are birthing prayers that have the power to break through."[3]

According to Cindy Jacobs, "prophetic intercession is an urging to pray given by the Holy Spirit.... You pray for the prayer requests that are on the heart of God. He nudges you to pray so that He can intervene.... God will direct you to pray to bring forth His will on the earth as it is His will in heaven."[4]   In other words, God says, *"Here is what I plan to do in that area, now prophesy it."*

Prophesying Our Destiny

Throughout the Bible we see examples of God's people making these types of prophetic declarations into situations in order to see His will come about. Such was the case in Ezekiel 36 and 37. God said to Ezekiel:

"But I had concern for My holy name, which the house of Israel had profaned among the nations wherever they went. Therefore say to the house of Israel, 'Thus says the Lord GOD: 'I do not do this for your sake, O house of Israel, but for My holy name's sake, which you have profaned among the nations wherever you went. And I will sanctify My great name, which has been profaned among the nations, which you have profaned in their midst; and the nations shall know that I am the LORD,' says the Lord GOD, 'when I am hallowed in you before their eyes. For I will take you from among the nations, gather you out of all countries, and bring you into your own land'" (Ezek. 36:21-24).

There was a process of scattering that had occurred among God's people. Satan knows how to scatter and he knows how to draw us into his process of division and scattering. So what the Lord told Ezekiel was that even though things had been scattered, He was going to bring them back together. God then gave Ezekiel an understanding of Israel's prophetic destiny that he was to declare into the earth:

"The hand of the LORD came upon me and brought me out in the Spirit of the LORD, and set me down in the midst of the valley; and it was full of bones. Then He caused me to pass by them all around, and behold, there were very many in the open valley; and indeed they were very dry. And He said to me, 'Son of man, can these bones live?' So I answered, 'O Lord GOD, You know' Again He said to me, 'Prophesy to these bones, and say to them, 'O dry bones, hear the word of the LORD! Thus says the Lord GOD to these bones: 'Surely I will cause breath to enter into you, and you shall live. I will put sinews on you and bring flesh upon you, cover you with skin and put breath in you; and you shall live. Then you shall know that I am the LORD'" (Ezek. 37:1-6).

There are four levels of prophetic declaration we see in Ezekiel 37 that help us understand the process of prophetic fulfillment. In each level there comes a place where the prophetic fulfillment has stalled. Understanding how the process stalls can help us proceed into the next dimension of prophetic fulfillment.

Level One Prophecy: Coming Together
"So I prophesied as I was commanded; and as I prophesied, there

was a noise, and suddenly a rattling; and the bones came together, bone to bone. Indeed, as I looked, the sinews and the flesh came upon them, and the skin covered them over;" (Ezek. 37:7-8a).

Ezekiel took the words that God gave him and declared them into the desolate situation that had overtaken Judah. That is what we mean by prophetic declaration. When Ezekiel declared God's will, action began to occur. The same is true with us. When we see God's prophetic destiny in our lives and begin to declare it, something will happen. We have to release faith before we see the results with our eyes. Sometimes we are looking for results without releasing faith, but it simply does not work that way. Faith comes first.

When Ezekiel first prophesied there was a rattling and the bones came together, and the sinews and flesh covered them. Therefore, we see in the first level of prophecy that when we are prophesying what God has promised us, we hear a new sound and see a new structure coming together. We even gain a portion of the plan to move forward. However, just having a plan is not enough.

Level Two Prophecy: The Breath of Life

"But there was no breath in them. Then He said to me, 'Prophesy to the breath, prophesy, son of man, and say to the breath, 'Thus says the Lord GOD: 'Come from the four winds, O breath, and breathe on these slain, that they may live'''" (Ezek. 37:8b-9).

Here we see the second level of prophecy. Ezekiel saw the bones come together and the flesh appear, but there was no breath. There was no life. Did that mean he was a false prophet? Of course not. It just meant that something was not yet working to produce prophetic fulfillment. So the Lord said, "Go back and prophesy to that part that has not received life." Notice, He did not tell Ezekiel to re-prophesy everything from the beginning, but only prophesy to the part that was not working and command it to come in line with God's plans and purposes.

When we encounter a snag in declaring God's word, it does not necessarily mean that we have not heard God or that we have failed. It often means that there is more and that we need to enter into a second level of prophecy in order to see life come into that which God is longing to accomplish.

Level Three Prophecy: Spiritual Warfare Over Hope Deferred

"So I prophesied as He commanded me, and breath came into them, and they lived, and stood upon their feet, an exceedingly great army. Then He said to me, 'Son of man, these bones are the whole house of Israel. They indeed say, 'Our bones are dry, our hope is lost, and we ourselves are cut off!'''" (Ezek. 37:10-11).

Ezekiel saw a great army result from his prophetic declarations. But as they began to speak they said that they were filled with lost hope. When we become filled with lost hope, it can easily deplete our faith for the future. Lost hope often works with rejection and causes us to feel isolated and cut off, as was the case with this great army. Furthermore, according to Proverbs 13:12, hope deferred makes the heart sick and releases a spirit of infirmity.

Ezekiel had seen great and miraculous things happen as a result of his prophetic declarations. Yet, there was hopelessness and infirmity. When this happens in our lives we need to enter into a third level of prophecy, which is spiritual warfare. It is not enough to have flesh and breath. We must fight against whatever the enemy is doing to try and steal the life that God has breathed into our destiny. If we don't go into spiritual warfare and overturn the enemy's plans to cause death, we won't progress and overturn a spirit of infirmity that has entered in and is resisting our prophetic fulfillment.

Much sickness is a result of hope deferred. There is a place in the fulfillment of the promise of God over our life where we have to deal with the past issues that have come against us to discourage and defeat us. Notice these bones had to express the hope deferred that was within them. Don't be afraid to face the problems of your past. By dealing with these past issues, we will be released to move into the hope for the future.

Level Four Prophecy: Hope for the Future

"Therefore prophesy and say to them, 'Thus says the Lord GOD: 'Behold, O My people, I will open your graves and cause you to come up from your graves, and bring you into the land of Israel. Then you shall know that I am the LORD, when I have opened your graves, O My people, and brought you up from your graves. I will put My Spirit in you, and you shall live, and I will place you in your own land. Then you shall know that I, the LORD, have spoken it and performed it,' says the LORD'" (Ezek. 37:12-14).

Notice that the phrase, "I will place you in your own land" was the prophetic destiny released in Ezekiel 36. The word of the Lord has come full circle! What if Ezekiel would have stopped pressing forward after the bones came together, but there was no breath? That's what we tend to do in the body of Christ. We think we've heard God, we prophesy, but when things don't turn out as we thought, we too often give up and end up falling short of reaching our prophetic destiny. We do not see the word that God has spoken to us manifesting and being fulfilled. As Ezekiel prophesied at the fourth level, resurrection power was released so that the graves could be opened and the people set in their own land. I love this phrase, "Then you will know that I, the Lord, have **spoken it** and **performed it**, says the Lord" (v. 14, emphasis added).

It's one thing for there to be a promise in your life that you know is from God, but it's another thing for that promise to be performed in your life. Four levels of agreement and prophesying were necessary to see the fulfillment of God's word here in Ezekiel. We cannot be a people that faint easily. Discouragement has no place in us as God's people. If we choose not to back up but to keep moving forward through the levels of prophecy, God will perform His will in us and bring about prophetic fulfillment!

Forty Days or Forty Years?

God has a cycle of life for each one of us. Our life cycle begins at conception and moves along in the following progression:

1. Conception, the beginning of God's purpose by knitting us together in the womb.
2. Birth, the bringing forth of the new life God has created.
3. Age of accountability with an awareness of our need for God.
4. Rebirth when we are quickened from darkness into light.
5. Receiving hope by searching for and receiving the expectation of God for our future.
6. Maturing of our faith into an overcoming weapon of God
7. Demonstration of God's power and wisdom that unlocks our destiny.
8. Manifestation of God's Glory and inner fulfillment of our identity in Him.
9. A completion of our role in the earth realm, facing death and entering into eternity.

The enemy loves to interrupt the life cycle in any one of these stages so that the fulfillment of our destiny cannot be completed. He would love for us to miss the *kairos* or opportune time that the Lord has in each of the phases above. If you miss that *now* time, it doesn't mean that things will never be back in order, it just means you postpone what God wants to do, and you enter into a prolonged wilderness season.

We all have wilderness seasons that are ordained of God where we are moving from one season to another. However, we can prolong this wilderness season. Jesus stayed in His wilderness season for 40 days, whereas the Israelites stayed in their wilderness season for 40 years. The Israelites were held captive in their wilderness season because of their unbelief and hardness of heart, whereas Jesus resisted the devil in His wilderness season and came out filled with power for His future.

The choice is ours! If we are willing to press toward our prophetic fulfillment in God's time, our season of desolation will not be prolonged. However, if we, like the Israelites, allow the enemy to overcome us with discouragement, hopelessness, and a lack of faith, we too may find ourselves in a prolonged season of desolation that leaves us wandering for many years.

As we mentioned at the beginning of this chapter, prophetic fulfillment can often seem to mess up our lives. In fact, we may even feel that everything has been turned upside down. But it is in the prophetic fulfillment that we reach God's destiny for our lives. As *you* come face to face with your own prophetic destiny in God's *now* time for your life, *you* must determine in your own heart if your wandering season will last for forty days or for forty years!

A Prophetic Declaration

Declarations have power! Here is a prophetic declaration for you to make that will help to unlock the next level of fulfillment of God's purpose in your life:

I declare that God has a purpose for my life. I receive wisdom and revelation over the hope of my calling. I declare that every strategy of hell that has interrupted God's plan for my life will be exposed. I declare that every hindrance that has stopped me from progressing will be revealed and I will advance in God's plan for my life. I declare my faith will be stirred. I declare new strength will come into my spirit. And I declare that the wilderness will blossom and God's glory will be seen in my life! I declare that the best is yet ahead!

Notes
[1] Dutch Sheets, *God's Timing for Your Life* (Ventura, CA: Regal Books, 2001), pp. 17, 18.
[2] Ibid., pp. 18-19.
[3] Barbara Wentroble, *Prophetic Intercession* (Ventura, CA: Renew, 1999), p. 27.
[4] Cindy Jacobs, *Possessing the Gates of the Enemy* (Tarrytown, NY: Chosen Books, 1991), pp. 146-147.

CHAPTER TWO

Seven Issues of
Prophetic Fulfillment

*For wisdom is better than rubies, and all the things
one may desire cannot be compared with her* (Prov. 8:11).

As we saw in the last chapter, prophetic fulfillment is not an
automatic occurrence in our lives. Of course God is sovereign and can do anything, but most of the time He does not override
the decisions we make for ourselves and, good or bad, we must live
with the consequences of those decisions. The wonderful thing
about the Lord is that even when we stray, if we listen He will
provide ways to get back into His ultimate plan. Therefore, we
must learn how to participate with His will for prophetic fulfillment to take place.

To fulfill is to bring something into actuality. This word also
means to carry out and order, to measure up, satisfy, bring to an
end, or complete. So prophetic fulfillment would mean that the
will and heart of God for our life, and all that He intends for us, is
completed. In other words, His desire for our life fully manifests.

In this chapter we will outline seven vital issues we need to understand that will help keep us on course as we move in God's full plan for our lives.

Issue One
You must know what God is saying to you, and then say, "yes and amen" to your promise.

"For all the promises of God in Him are Yes, and in Him Amen, to the glory of God through us" (2 Cor. 1:20). Sadly, many Christians will die without ever having fulfilled their prophetic destinies; and it may not be because of sin in their lives. Often it will be because they never learned to hear God's voice and understand where He was trying to lead. Therefore, they end up groping in the dark unable to obey the Lord because they do not comprehend what He is requiring in order for them to move toward their destinies.

Even if we have a good idea of where God wants us to move, the path toward that destination is usually very different than we imagined. Countless times I have heard comments such as, "I knew God would do this, but I never imagined it would be this way!" That is why it is so important for us to hear God at every step along the way.

One key principle for saying **yes and amen** to your promise is continuing to look forward rather than looking back. Hanging on to what has already slipped away from us accomplishes nothing and can even cloud our vision of what lies ahead. Many people lose their sense of moving toward their future because they hang on to their past. For true prophetic fulfillment, we have to grab onto what God is doing now. We need to say, "Lord, what are You doing with me *today*? What are You trying to move me into so I can reconnect and bring about that which You are trying to do for my future?"

Once we have come into an understanding of our promises, we

need to acknowledge it with **yes and amen**. That means we need to actually verbalize it to God and to others. "For it is with your heart that you believe and are justified, and it is with your mouth that you confess and are saved" (Rom. 10:10, NIV). From this verse we see that the confession of our mouth is tremendously important. The word confess in this verse means harmonious or together. Therefore, by verbalizing God's promises for us, we are actually coming into harmonious agreement together with Him. This act does a great deal toward building our faith and shutting the door to Satan's lies.

What comes out of our mouths is vitally important. "Not what goes into the mouth defiles a man; but what comes out of the mouth, this defiles a man" (Matt. 15:11). This verse, along with Romans 10:10, shows us that we have both the power of salvation and the power of defilement in the words we choose to speak. Our confessions could mean the difference between prophetic fulfillment or missing our destiny. For this reason we must come into agreement by verbalizing "yes" and "amen" to God's promises for us.

We want to be quick to add one note of caution when it comes to verbalizing what we believe are God's promises for us. We must be careful to let the Lord give us wisdom over who to tell and what to say, otherwise we may very likely end up in a mess, just as Joseph did when he bragged about his dream to his brothers who were so angry they sold him into slavery! It is often a matter of timing. Broadcasting something that is meant to be kept on a shelf or in a prayer closet is the spiritual equivalent of the old wartime adage, "lose lips sinks ships"!

Issue Two
The promise that God has for you must be incorporated into the overall destiny for you and for others.

"And if one member suffers, all the members suffer with it; or if one member is honored, all the members rejoice with it" (1 Cor. 12:26). God does nothing independently of whatever else He is trying to accomplish. In other words, whatever He is trying to do in your life, fits into a bigger picture.

In a society such as ours that places high value on individual achievement, it is often hard for us to understand that our destiny is linked to others, and that we will not succeed alone. We are connected one to another. Therefore, the promise God has for you is being incorporated into a greater destiny of which you are a part. Your promise is linked to the overall movement of God, not only in your life, but in your territory, and in the generations past and yet to come. Even though God is a very personal God, He enacts our promises along with those of others to whom He has connected us. If we or they aren't asking God to work out our promises, we all suffer. This is an issue we will discuss in greater detail in Chapter Five.

Issue Three
We must be in a process of receiving prophetic revelation.

Our life and destiny is on a continuum. As we move through life, we need to constantly seek new direction and new revelation from God. We can't just grab a hold of one level of revelation and think that's going to ride us through to the end. In the last chapter we discussed the four levels of prophecy that Ezekiel had to move through in order to see God accomplish all that He intended to in the valley of dry bones. If Ezekiel had stopped at any point before God's full purpose had been accomplished, he would have failed. Ezekiel went through a four-step process at each new level of prophecy. These four steps are the same ones we need to follow if we are going to stay on track with prophetic fulfillment in our own lives:

1. He received prophetic revelation. Ezekiel sought God and was open to receiving prophetic instruction. In fact, he *expected*

God to speak to him. How often in our daily lives do we *expect* to hear God? God is speaking to us today! We need to learn how to listen for God's voice and direction in our lives in order to receive the instructions that will move us forward.

2.   He obeyed the voice of the Lord. God told Ezekiel what to say and do in order for the next step to be accomplished. This seems so basic, and yet it is a critical step that we must understand. Ezekiel could not have moved to the fourth level of prophecy with-out first obeying God at the first, second, and third levels. If you are having difficulty gaining new revelation and hearing the voice of the Lord, go back and be sure you have done all that the Lord has re-quired of you thus far. For example, if we have fallen out of relationship with someone, and the Lord reveals to us that we have to go get right with that person, we should not go back to the Lord looking for new revelation until we have

> If you are having difficulty gaining new revelation and hearing the voice of the Lord, go back and be sure you have done all that the Lord has required of you thus far.

obeyed Him in the last revelation. If we want to continue to move forward toward prophetic fulfillment, we'd better go get right with that person.

3.   He watched God's purpose being accomplished and as-sessed the situation. At each level of obedience, Ezekiel saw miracles happen as God's will was accomplished. Even so, he knew that all of God's purposes had not yet been fulfilled. He saw the bones come together. This in itself must have been a great and miraculous sight. But when he looked closer, he saw that even with this great miracle, there was no breath. Then he saw breath come into them. A great army of living, breathing beings replaced a dead pile of dry, useless bones. And yet there was hopelessness and infirmity. It was not until Ezekiel saw the Lord break infirmity and death off of the great army and bring them into the land He had promised them that the process of prophetic fulfillment was complete. Even though we may see great miracles along the way, we need to be sensitive to the Holy Spirit's leading as to whether or not His will has been fully accomplished.

 4. He listened for his next instruction. Miracle after miracle did not stop Ezekiel from seeking God for the next step. He did not bask in the awesome works of God in a way that stopped Him from looking forward. Of course we need to stop and thank God for His great power and allow ourselves to be drawn into worship. But, we can't let the glory of something that has already occurred keep us from moving toward a greater level of glory.

 Have you ever tried walking backwards as you focus on where you have just been? Not only is your progress greatly slowed, but you are liable to fall on an obstacle that you should have seen. Remember, Jesus "set his face like a flint towards Jerusalem" (Luke 9:51). He never got off track in His purposes on Earth, and by staying totally focused He brought redemption to us. We need to keep our eyes focused on what lies ahead and seek God for our next instruction. Even with all of Paul's great accomplishments for the Lord he writes, "I do not count myself to have apprehended; but one thing I do, forgetting those things which are behind and reaching forward to those things which are ahead, I press toward the goal for the prize of the upward call of God in Christ Jesus" (Phil. 3:13-14). Paul was reaching toward his prophetic fulfillment.

Issue Four
We must learn to do warfare with our prophecies.

"This charge I commit to you, son Timothy, according to the prophecies previously made concerning you, that by them you may wage the good warfare" (1 Tim. 1:18). Receiving a prophetic revelation from God about what He wants to accomplish does not mean that it's a done deal. There is a conditional nature to prophecy that involves both our obedience and our willingness to "war" with a word. Because this is such a critical issue in prophetic fulfillment, we have devoted all of Chapter Three to the subject of warfare.

Issue Five
We must have our authority and accountability structures in place for prophetic fulfillment.

The issue of proper authority and alignments in our lives cannot be omitted or even understated when it comes to prophetic fulfillment. This biblical principle is brought up over and over again in topics such as parents over children, masters over slaves, employers over employees, the priesthood over the people, and so forth. Watchman Nee said it this way: "We should not be occupied with right or wrong, good or evil; rather should we know who is the authority above us. Once we learn to whom we must be subject, we naturally find our place in the body. Alas, how many Christians today have not the faintest idea concerning subjection. No wonder there is so much confusion and disorder.... Obedience is a foundational principle. If this matter of authority remains unsolved, nothing can be solved. As faith is the principle by which we obtain life, so obedience is the principle by which that life is lived out."[1]

We will never reach prophetic fulfillment as loners. Even though you can be right with God and end up in heaven, lack of understanding authority won't bring fulfillment on earth. If we are to be victorious in our lives, we cannot sidestep the Bible. Therefore, we need to understand the role that authority plays in our lives. Here are some important factors in being properly aligned under the authority God has placed in our lives:

1. Mentoring. Despite the fact that my earthly father was not a good representation of the Lord, God has always seen to it that there have been spiritual fathers in my life who have provided mentoring and guidance for me. After my dad died, He put a natural uncle in my life. Then my mother met a wonderful man who later became my stepfather and gave me clear direction to attend Texas A&M University. Then He put a key pastor in my life, then a mission leader, and now a wonderful apostolic leader that I am aligned with, C. Peter Wagner. I have always coveted these relationships and have submitted to them.

But not all authority in my life has been from men. There have been many women in my life whom I also consider spiritual authorities and to whom I submit. My mother and grandmother were certainly in that category. God placed a godly woman named LaCelia Henderson in my life after I got baptized in the Holy Spirit to teach me spiritual life. In more recent years I have had the privilege of being mentored by Doris Wagner, a wonderful administrator, as I have served under her at Global Harvest Ministries. All those who have mentored me, both men and women, have played crucial roles in my own prophetic fulfillment.

2. Discipline. Submitting to authority always brings discipline into our lives. In this context we are not using the word to mean punishment, but rather an inward strength and a pathway by which God can work in our lives. In his classic book *Celebration of Discipline*, Richard J. Foster says, "God has given us [discipline] of spiritual life as a means of receiving his grace. [Discipline] allows us to place ourselves before God so that he can transform us."[2]   My brother, Keith, simply puts it this way: "Discipline defines the gift."

3. Freedom. Foster goes on to say, "I said that every Discipline has its corresponding freedom. What freedom corresponds to submission? It is the ability to lay down the terrible burden of always needing to get our own way. The obsession to demand that things go the way we want them to go is one of the greatest bondages of human society... In submission we are at last free to value other people. Their dreams and plans become important to us... For the first time we can love people unconditionally."[3]

As we said earlier, our prophetic destinies are always linked to what God is working to accomplish in the lives of those with whom we are connected, in the territories in which we live, and in the generations to come. As we submit to authority, we have the freedom to see God's bigger plan and understand the part we are called to play.

I love this verse: "And now look, I free you this day from the chains that were on your hand. If it seems good to you to come with me to Babylon, come, and I will look after you. But if it seems wrong for you to come with me to Babylon, remain here. See, all the land is before you; wherever it seems good and convenient for you to go, go there" (Jer. 40:4). In other words, after Jeremiah had done what the Lord had asked him to do, he was granted the freedom to choose where he would go in days ahead. The word freedom means to open wide, loosen, release, untie, unshackle, or liberate. It often refers to opening one's hand, eyes, or mouth. Understanding authority in our lives does indeed bring freedom.

4. Order. Everything God has created has order. One of Satan's chief goals is to counteract the works of God by thwarting His order. Therefore, Satan works to bring disunity, mistrust, confusion, disobedience, ineffectiveness, and ultimately destruction by breaking down God's structure of authority. As we choose to submit to God's authority structures in our lives, we restore and maintain God's plan of order, and make great strides toward prophetic fulfillment.

God has a prototype of order for the church. First Corinthians 12:28 says, "And God has appointed these in the church: first apostles, second prophets, third teachers, and after that miracles…" This verse does not mean that each gift does not operate in its own authority. However, it does mean that until they are properly aligned we will not see God's model of what He has in heaven manifest on earth. That's how order works. Once we come into order, which is a military term, we are aligned properly for victory.

5. Covering. Covering means protection, concealing, warmth, hidden from view, or being in a place of safety. Being in proper alignment with authority produces these things in our lives. If we have not moved out from under our place of authority, the enemy has far fewer available means of attacking us because we are covered or hidden from his view. Psalm 91 is a beautiful example of covering as we remain under the authority of the Lord: "He who dwells in the secret place of the Most High shall abide under the shadow of the Almighty. I will say of the LORD, 'He is my refuge and my fortress; my God, in Him I will trust.' Surely He shall deliver you from the snare of the fowler and from the perilous pestilence. He shall cover you with His feathers, and under His wings you shall take refuge; his truth shall be your shield and buckler. You shall not be afraid of the terror by night, nor of the arrow that flies by day" (vv. 1-4).

6. Clarity. God often gives those in authority over us a supernatural insight into our lives. Their wisdom and counsel can provide the clarity of vision to move forward that we may not possess in and of ourselves. We, of course, need to weigh advice with the discernment God has given to us, and we need to be careful of those that may be trying to abuse their authority by controlling us. Nevertheless, we must be open to receiving God's clarity and wisdom through our authority structures.

7. Connections. Many times our destiny does not come about because we are not connected properly to others in the body of Christ. As we quoted before, Watchman Nee said, "Once we learn to whom we must be subject, we naturally find our place in the body."[4] We see incredible connections in the Bible that brought about the fulfillment of God's purposes. Deborah and Barak are one example. Then Esther and Mordecai are another. In the New Testament we see Paul and Barnabas. We see that Peter's destiny was fulfilled by Andrew connecting him with Jesus. Jesus then began to prophesy into Peter's life the full redemption plan God had for him (see John 1:51).

God's prophetic purpose for our lives and for territories requires us to be connected to one another. We need to know with whom God has sovereignly linked us, maintain strong alliances with those people, and respect those in authority. Understanding and maintaining proper connections is another way to destroy Satan's schemes because he will have a difficult time infiltrating our ranks.

8. Healing. "Is anyone among you sick? Let him call for the elders of the church, and let them pray over him, anointing him with oil in the name of the Lord" (James 5:14). During the season when my wife, Pam, was being healed of barrenness, there came a time when she went to our pastor and asked that he pray for her, which he did. I honestly believe that the barrenness would not have been broken off of her if she had not been obedient to the Bible's admonition in James 5. When she submitted herself to biblical authority by asking for prayer, it started a progression of events in motion that liberated and healed her.

9. Faith. In our book *The Future War of the Church* (Renew), we explained the link between authority and faith: "The Lord showed me that if I would begin to understand and analyze every authority that had influence in my life, I would begin to operate in a new level of faith. Faith is linked with authority. To the extent that we submit to the authority God has placed in our lives, our faith has the opportunity to be stretched and strengthened. Faith is the overcoming agent that God's people have on this Earth (see John 14:12); therefore, if the Church is to overcome, we must understand and submit to proper authority."[5]

10. Power. Being in proper alignment with authority, both those in authority over you and those to whom you are an authority, is a key to power. In Matthew 8 we see the story of the centurion who pled with Jesus to heal his sick servant. "The centurion answered and said, 'Lord, I am not worthy that You should come under my roof. But only speak a word, and my servant will be healed. For I also am a man under authority, having soldiers under me'" (Matt. 8:8-9). This centurion was able to seek out the Lord and gain healing for his servant because he submitted to the Lord's authority and used his own authority to ask for someone underneath him. His understanding of where he stood in the authority structure gave him power to help those under him.

Issue Six
We must have a persevering spirit to break through.

Prophetic fulfillment is a process—sometimes a very long process that can test our ability to persevere and believe that God will do all that He promised. Hell doesn't want you to break through. It takes perseverance to break through the processes of hell that have been set against your promise and your destiny. Therefore, I always try to stay close to God so that I can persevere in those hard times. I love the way my dear friend Barbara Yoder describes persevering for breakthrough in her book, *The Breaker Anointing*:

"God has a great deal for us to possess, but it will take great faith and perseverance. God is continually putting new conquests before us to develop our faith and perseverance at a higher level. We must continually remind ourselves of what God instructed the Israelites in Judges 3:1-4. He said: 'Now these are the nations which the LORD left, that He might test Israel by them, that is, all who had not known any of the wars in Canaan (this was only so that the generations of the children of Israel might be taught to know war, at least those who had not formerly known it), namely, five lords of the Philistines, all the Canaanites, the Sidonians, and the Hivites who dwelt in Mount Lebanon, from Mount Baal Hermon to the entrance of Hamath. And they were left, that He might test Israel by them, to know whether they would obey the commandments of the LORD, which He had commanded their fathers by the hand of Moses.'

"We can also decide we want to quit at some point because a gate seems too hard or too unconquerable. We may be tired and weary of the battle. We want to sit down, take a rest, and check out. We have the option of sitting down and living a life of ease. But by doing so we will never reach our potential because fear or weariness overtook us at the threshold. Some make this decision and fail to reach their destiny.

"Paul said that he kept pressing on to attain that which he was intended to attain (see Phil. 3:12-14). God apprehended Paul not just to convert him but also to use Paul to accomplish a great ministry, to take the gospel to the Gentiles in many nations. Paul pressed through despite many trials."[6]

Issue Seven
Prophetic fulfillment requires humility.

As we have seen all throughout this chapter, we will not reach our destinies apart from one another. We are dependant on each other for prophetic fulfillment. There is no room for pride in the equation. It also keeps us humble knowing that unless God infuses us with strength, power, and wisdom, we cannot break forth. God is only going to use humble, holy people to build His kingdom in days ahead.

In a recent teaching that C. Peter Wagner delivered on humility, he quoted Andrew Murray, "We need only think for a moment what faith is. Is it not the confession of nothingness and helplessness, the surrender and the waiting to let God work? Is it not in itself the most humbling thing there can be—the acceptance of our place as dependents, who can claim or get or do nothing but what grace bestows?"[7]

We can never reach our destiny, nor even draw our next breath, apart from the grace and mercy of God. No matter what our prophetic promises may be, let us never come to the place of forgetting that we are only dust that has experienced the touch of God. It is only through Him, and through those with whom He has connected us that we will ever accomplish the purpose for which He fashioned us!

Notes
[1] Watchman Nee, *Spiritual Authority* (New York: Christian Fellowship Publishers, Inc., 1972), p. 23.
[2] Richard J. Foster, *Celebration of Discipline* (San Francisco, CA: Harper and Row, Publishers, 1988), p. 7.
[3] Ibid., pp. 111-112.
[4] Nee, p. 23.
[5] Chuck D. Pierce and Rebecca Wagner Sytsema, *The Future War of the Church* (Ventura, CA: Renew Books, 2001), p. 32.
[6] Barbara Yoder, *The Breaker Anointing* (Colorado Springs, CO: Wagner Publications, 2001), pp 55-56.
[7] Andrew Murray, *Humility* (New Kensington PA: Whitaker House, 1982), p. 68.

CHAPTER THREE

Warring with a Prophetic Word

*This charge I commit to you, son Timothy, according to the
prophecies previously made concerning you, that by them you
may wage the good warfare* (1 Tim. 1:18).

U p to this point, we have talked a great deal about destiny and
prophetic fulfillment, but we have not discussed prophecy itself. This chapter is devoted to understanding the role that prophecy
plays in our lives, and how to wage warfare with the prophecies we
receive.

Understanding Personal Prophecy

The simple definition of prophecy is speaking forth the mind and
heart of God under the inspiration of the Holy Spirit. Therefore, to
give an accurate word of God we must have both His mind and
emotion as we deliver that word. A prophetic declaration commu-
nicates God's intent to fulfill His promises to us. Receiving a

prophetic word can have a powerful impact on the perception of our prophetic destiny. This word can help shape our vision for the future and bring us into a deeper understanding of God's heart for our lives.

In our book *Receiving the Word of the Lord*, we discuss more fully the value, process, and function of prophecy, and offer several ways to test a prophetic word. That book will help anyone needing a basic explanation of personal prophecy. In the context of this book, however, we want to focus on prophecy as it pertains to prophetic fulfillment. To do that, we need to take a closer look at several aspects of how prophecy works in our lives:[1]

Prophecy is Incomplete

"For we know in part and we prophesy in part" (1 Cor. 13:9). No personal or corporate word of prophecy is complete in and of itself. In his excellent book, *Developing Your Prophetic Gifting*, Graham Cooke says, "God only reveals what we need to know in order to do his will in that particular time and place. The things that he does not wish us to know, he keeps secret from the one prophesying. Elisha said, 'The Lord has hidden it from me!' (2 Kings 4:27). In other words, 'I don't know.'"[2]

Cooke goes on to say, "Oddly enough, a prophecy will give us positive highlights about our future role or tasks, but may say nothing about any pitfalls we may encounter. It may not refer to enemy opposition, people letting us down, or any crushing disappointments that we may experience as we attempt to be faithful to our call."[3]

God may give us a little bit here and a little bit there. In retrospect, we may wonder why God didn't tell us this or that, or why He did tell us some seemingly unimportant detail. God always knows what He is doing when He reveals His heart to us through prophecy. That is something that we must simply trust. We must bear in mind, however, that we do not know all we may encounter, or how the prophecies may be fulfilled. Prophecy may point out a path, but we must follow the Lord daily and trust in Him as we move ahead along that path. Prophetic fulfillment comes in moving down the path that was pointed out through personal prophecy.

Prophecy Evolves

As we follow the Lord in obedience, He will give us our next piece. He will not tell us what He wants us to do three steps down the road. He gives it to us step by step. Such was the case with Abraham. God gave him a piece here and a piece there. Each time Abraham obeyed, God would speak to him again. God would confirm, expand, give new insights, and move Abraham on to his next place. One exciting dimension of Abraham's prophetic evolution comes in Genesis 22 when God reveals Himself as Jehovah Jireh to Abraham. This name of God actually means that God will reveal provision that we can't see so we can advance into our future. Another tremendous concept in this chapter was that God prophesied the next piece of Abraham's destiny into his son Isaac. Therefore, what Abraham could not accomplish or complete was passed on to the next generation.

That is the way of prophecy. Each prophetic word is incomplete, yet as we are faithful to obey God, we receive new pieces of the puzzle. Prophecies will often build on earlier prophecies to bring confirmation and fresh understanding. Cooke writes, "The Lord will never speak the totality of his heart to us in a single prophetic word. Rather he speaks words that will give us a focus for now and the immediate future. As we work within those prophecies and allow our lives to be encouraged and shaped by them, we can see that prophecy builds from one word to another."[4]

Prophecy is Conditional

The key to the process of prophecy is obedience. God will not usurp our wills and force us to follow His will. Mary, for instance, could have said no to the prophetic pronouncement that she would become pregnant. Instead, she responded by saying, "Behold the maidservant of the Lord! Let it be to me according to your word" (Luke 1:38). Had she said no, the Holy Spirit would never have forced her to become pregnant! Although she did not completely understand how this would happen, nor did she grasp the magnitude of what she had been chosen for, nevertheless, she knew that through the prophetic word, God had revealed His destiny for her life. Through her choice of obedience, the word came to pass and the human race gained access to its full redemptive plan.

The condition of obedience to the Holy Spirit is not a negotiable factor in prophetic fulfillment. In the Old Testament the word "faith" is used only twice. However, we find that the concept of faith is built in to the obedience of God's people based upon the promise that God has spoken to them. As these people obeyed, they became the fathers and mothers of our faith. Therefore, when God's word comes to you always look for the obedience factor.

As we said in the last chapter, just because we have received a prophetic word does not mean it's a done deal. We are often tempted to believe that the fulfillment of a prophetic word is the next step in our lives, but there may be some things we have to do first in obedience to God. Abraham, for instance, had to be circumcised before he saw prophetic fulfillment. And then there was that big event where he had to put Isaac, his only son, on the altar. "Only son" meant that his entire future was wrapped up in this individual. However, that was the condition God had placed on him before He could reveal and extend His promise to the next generation.

Let us add one note of clarification: There is some prophecy that is unconditional and that God alone will fulfill. God is sovereign. He can do anything He wishes. But usually in His plan He has made it provisional for us to come into agreement with His sovereign hand. Therefore the words that He chooses to sovereignly accomplish are usually pertaining to the human race as a whole, rather than personal prophecy. This does not remove His sovereign grace to intervene at any time in our life, but it keeps us actively pursuing Him.

Prophecy Has Timing

We must understand the seasons of God and not move out of His timing. In Chapter One we talked about God's *now* times in our lives. Not every prophetic word is given in a *now* time. The prophecy that Daniel uncovered for the children of Israel had to lie dormant for 70 years before its time came!

One of the first prophetic words that ever came over my life was: "You will have an anointing to know God's times and seasons. You will move supernaturally in His timing." I had no idea what this word meant. If there has been one anointing God has taught me in my life, it's this one. This anointing has been called by many the Issachar anointing (see 1 Chron. 12:32).

Receiving a word about a future ministry might not mean that we run off and start moving in that direction the next day. In misplaced enthusiasm, many people might start doing what they were eventually supposed to do, but because they moved out of God's season, they will never be as effective as if they had waited on the Lord. It is like a baby who is born prematurely. That child may be alive, but will have many more weaknesses, complications, and developmental obstacles to overcome, and may never reach the potential it would have had it been carried to full term. We need to be sensitive to God's development—of training, mentoring, and circumstances in our lives that will provide the fertile soil where prophetic fulfillment will blossom to its fullest.

By the same token, we need to know when to move with a prophetic word. When I first met Rebecca Sytsema, she was single. She had promises from the Lord about her husband, but had not yet met him. In 1994 several of us were preparing to go to a spiritual warfare conference. Rebecca shared with me she had had a dream that she was going to meet her husband at that conference. I immediately knew that was right. We got on the phone to make her a hotel reservation, but the receptionist told us there was no room available.

Without hesitation I said to the hotel worker, "You must find her a room! Her husband is waiting for her there!" Without any explanation of what I meant by my statement, the people at the hotel were able to find a room. It was at that conference that Rebecca met Jack Sytsema. Two years later I performed their wedding ceremony, and they have since had three children and are on a solid path toward all that God has for them in their lives. But what if she had not gone to the conference? I can't say that she would never have met Jack, but she would have missed a *now* season and had to wait longer than God intended to move toward prophetic fulfillment.

This should give great encouragement to those waiting on a similar promise. God has the times and seasons worked out. Do not run ahead of God, but be prepared to move when the time comes!

The Dangers of Presumption

Besides moving out of God's timing, there are other dangers we can encounter with personal prophecy if we move in presumption. In other words, we receive a prophecy and, rather than allowing the Lord to work it out in our lives, we presume we know exactly what the prophecy means and try to make it happen. The word may be accurate, but the interpretation can get us moving in the wrong direction. Jesus overcame the spirit of presumption in the wilderness. Satan would quote Scripture to Him and try and get Him to act on it. But Jesus defied Satan's attempts to get Him moving out of God's timing.

. The enemy does not care which end of the continuum he uses to get you into unbelief. He can use doubt and hardness of heart to keep you from moving forward, or he can use presumption to get you to move forward out of season. When we move in presumption, we open up ourselves and our families to needless attacks from the enemy. We need to be careful not to presume when and how God intends to bring prophetic fulfillment. We must remember that we only see a part of the picture. The way to avoid the pitfall of presumption is to obey the Lord in what you know you need to do next. In her book *The Voice of God*, Cindy Jacobs offers the following list of questions to help us stay out of presumption when we are ready to make changes based on a word or prophecy:

♦ Is this consistent with everything God has been saying about my life?

♦ How will this affect my current responsibilities? For example, will I be able to take care of my family financially? What kind of stress will this put on my family? Are they willing to sacrifice what will be required if I make these changes in my life?

♦ Have I reached a maturity level in my life that will enable me to perform with integrity the new tasks and/or changes, or will I flake out because I am not properly prepared?

♦ Do brothers and sisters in the Lord witness to this word, especially those in authority over me?[5]

Going to War

Having given some basic issues that are important for us to understand when it comes to personal prophecy, let's look at the spiritual
warfare often necessary to see prophecy fulfilled. Just as God has a
plan for your life, you can be just as sure that Satan also has a plan
for your life. Satan considers it his job to thwart every plan and
purpose God has for you, for your family, and for your territory.
That is the very essence of spiritual warfare—whose plan will pre-
vail?

First Timothy 1:18-19 says, "Timothy, my son, I give you this
instruction in keeping with the prophecies once made about you, so
that by following them you may fight the good fight, holding on to
faith and a good conscience. Some have rejected these and so have
shipwrecked their faith" (NIV).

Do you have a prophetic promise concerning your children, but
they are not making wise choices? Do you have prophetic promises
concerning ministry, finances, future direction, barrenness breaking off your life, or any number of other things? Keeping in mind
all we have discussed in this chapter concerning obedience, timing,
presumption, and prophetic evolution, ask the Lord if the enemy is
at work to keep you from prophetic fulfillment. If so, it's time to go
to war! As Jim Goll puts it, "Once you have secured an authentic
prophetic promise, load it, take aim and shoot! Fight the fight and
wage war with the prophetic."[6]

Praying a Prophetic Word

God's word has tremendous power. Remember that it was by His
word alone that He created light: "Then God *said*, 'Let there be
light'; and there was light" (Gen. 1:3, italics added). By His word
alone He created day and night, the earth and the heavens, land and
sea, vegetation and every living creature. Everything that has been
created exists because of the word of God. Furthermore, we see in

John 1 that Jesus is the Word of God, "In the beginning was the Word, and the Word was with God, and the Word was God.... And the Word became flesh and dwelt among us, and we beheld His glory, the glory as of the only begotten of the Father, full of grace and truth" (John 1:1,14). God's Word, therefore, not only gives us our being, but provides our redemption and secures our future through Christ.

When God speaks a prophetic promise, there is power within the words. There is power to gain the supply we need. There is power to step into a new level of faith. And there is power to overthrow the enemy. Couple with that the fact that our own words have a certain measure of power in

> As we gain each victory in the war over prophetic fulfillment, God releases a new anointing of authority on us that gives us even greater power to overthrow our enemy in the battles that lie ahead.

them. Our words have the power to both bless and curse (see James 3:9). Proverbs 18:21 says that life and death are in the power of the tongue. Our words spoken in prayer can move the very hand of God and can block Satan's destructive maneuvers. Therefore, when we take a prophetic word that God has given us and speak it back to God in prayer, it is a potent combination.

Jim Goll reminds us, "At times we must declare the [prophetic] word to our circumstances and any mountain of opposition standing in the way. We remind ourselves of the promise that lies ahead, and we remind the devil and command any foul spirits—for example, the spirit of discouragement—to back off, declaring what the written and spoken promises of God reveal. Each of us has purposes, promises and a destiny to find, fight for and fulfill. So take your 'Thus saith the Lord' to battle with you and fight."[7]

What Are We Warring Against?

There are five areas we see from the Word of God where we are in conflict:

1. The devil. Satan and his demons affect most of us. This includes Christians. He has a hierarchy and a horde underneath him that are confederated to stop the purposes of God.

2. The flesh. The flesh tries to hang on for dear life instead of submitting to the power of the cross and being crucified. Galatians 5:24 says we should crucify our flesh each day. The flesh hinders us from obeying God. Without this daily crucifixion, we give the devil the right to tempt and ensnare us.

3. Enemies. Many times evil spirits will embed in individuals or groups of individuals collectively. Then they use these individuals to set themselves against God's covenant plan in a person's life.

4. The world. The world system is organized and is usually competing contrary to God's will. We are enemies of the world. The god of this world is controlling the world system. Though we are not part of this world's system, we still live in it. The world system has both a religious aspect as well as a governmental aspect that must be understood if we are going to successfully maneuver in the world but never be part of the world.

5. Death. Death is our final enemy. Jesus overcame death and we must war with the strategies of death until we have completed our life cycle in the Earth. And through His Spirit we can also overcome.

If we do not war these things we will never possess the inheritance God has given us.

A War Strategy

Because of what we are warring against, we must have a war strategy for our life. In addition to the power of praying a prophetic word back to God, the Bible has many other warfare strategies when it comes to prophetic fulfillment. One excellent example of this is in 2 Chronicles 20. In this story a number of Judah's enemies came together to form a confederation against Judah and were planning to invade their God-ordained, God-promised boundaries. In obedience to the Lord, Judah had not previously invaded those who were in the confederation and who were now arising to steal what rightfully belonged to Judah. There was no question that the combined strength of their enemies could easily have overthrown them.

Jehoshaphat, who was a godly king, cried out to the Lord for a strategy for the warfare they faced. As he addressed the people he said, "Believe in the Lord your God, and you shall be established; believe His prophets, and you shall prosper" (2 Chron. 20:20). He called the nation together and followed these steps:

1. They fasted (v. 3). One of the greatest weapons we have in spiritual warfare is fasting. In *Possessing Your Inheritance* we said, "Fasting is a discipline that most religions and cults understand because this sacrifice releases power. For the Christian, fasting is essential. Often you cannot gain the revelation you need for your next step without it…. Fasting removes spiritual clutter and positions us to receive from God. By fasting, we make it possible for the Lord to more powerfully reveal Himself to us—not because He speaks more clearly when we fast, but because we can hear Him more clearly."[8]

2. They inquired of the Lord (v. 4). This was a strategy David often used when he was about to be overthrown by his enemies. Each time David inquired of the Lord, he received strategic revelation that led to victory. Like David and like the people of Judah, when we are at war and we inquire of the Lord, we should expect Him to answer in a way that will provide strategy and direction for us.

3. In faith they declared their God-given boundaries reminding God of His promises of inheritance to them (v. 7). As we described above, they prayed the prophecy back to God, and they did so in faith. They let their faith arise. Faith is that pause between knowing what God's plan is and seeing it actually take place.[9] According to Jim Goll, "Take any promises that have been spoken to you by the Holy Spirit and turn them into persistent prayer, reminding God of His word…. Use these confirmed, authentic words from heaven to create faith within your heart. Let them pave the way for the entrance of ever-increasing faith in your life."[10]

4. They acknowledged their own futility, and recognized that they needed to keep their eyes on God or be overtaken by the enemy (v. 12). Even though we may feel powerless and helpless in the face of Satan's onslaughts, we need to remember that our perspective is very different from God's. If we focus purely on our circumstances, Satan can use what we see with our eyes to bring discouragement, hopelessness, rob our joy, and cause us to be overtaken by fear. But when we keep our eyes on the Lord, we can transcend our circumstances by quieting our hearts and minds and focusing on the Lord and His promises. Psalm 25:15 says, "My eyes are ever toward the LORD, for He shall pluck my feet out of the net."

5. They positioned themselves to face the enemy (v. 17). Positioning is a crucial element of any warfare. If we are not in position when the enemy comes, he can easily overtake us. We must, therefore, be sure that we are in full obedience to all the Lord has required of us, and that we are walking on the path He has set for us. Then, donning the full armor of God, we will be ready to face the enemy when he attacks. We, therefore, need to ask ourselves, are we standing where we need to be? Do we need to change course or direction to get into the right position?

6. They sought counsel (v. 21). It is vitally important for us to be surrounded by those who can give us wise counsel. Satan is such a master of deception that if we are standing alone, we can easily fall into deception. I have often heard Cindy Jacobs say, "if you don't think you can be deceived, then you already are!" If you are not under spiritual authority to those who are wise in the ways of God and routinely asking for their counsel, ask the Lord to bring you to that place before moving on in warfare.

7. They worshiped and praised the Lord (v. 22). There is, perhaps, no stronger weapon of warfare than praise and worship to the Lord. Satan hates our worship to God for many reasons. For one, he is jealous of our worship. He longs to obtain it for himself through whatever means he can. For another, he knows that the weapon of worship is strong and effective. Consider the words of Psalm 149:5-9:

"Let the saints be joyful in glory; let them sing aloud on their beds. Let the high praises of God be in their mouth, and a two-edged sword in their hand, to execute vengeance on the nations, and punishments on the peoples; to bind their kings with chains, and their nobles with fetters of iron; to execute on them the written judgment—this honor have all His saints. Praise the LORD!"

Another important reason is explained by Cindy Jacobs, "When we praise God, He inhabits or enters our praises, and His power overwhelms the power of the enemy. He is a mighty God, and Satan cannot match His strength. Light will dispel the darkness through God's entering into our praise."[11] Through praise, the Lord Himself begins to do warfare on our behalf to silence our enemy, as we shall see.

The Victory

In this story of Jehoshaphat we find the passage, "Stand still and see the salvation of the LORD" (v. 17). As the people of Judah earnestly sought the Lord and followed the strategy the He gave them, the Scripture says that they were to stand still and allow the Lord to battle on their behalf. In the end, it was the Lord who set ambushes against the enemy so that they were utterly destroyed. Verse 24 says that not one of their enemies escaped!

The Lord will do the same for us. We must seek the Lord, be obedient to His commands, and let Him handle the rest for us: "'Not by might nor by power, but by My Spirit,' says the LORD of hosts" (Zech. 4:6). If we are to have prophetic fulfillment in our lives, we have no choice but to believe that God will do what He said He will do!

The Spoils of War

This story does not end with the victory of the people of Judah against their enemies. There is something more that we need to grasp. Their victory was not complete until they gathered the spoils of war. Verse 25 says, "When Jehoshaphat and his people came to take away their spoil, they found among them an abundance of valuables on the dead bodies, and precious jewelry, which they stripped off for themselves, more than they could carry away; and they were three days gathering the spoil because there was so much."

Can you imagine so many dead bodies covered in so much wealth that it took the people of Judah a full three days to collect it all—and it was more than they could carry away? God saw to it that their enemy was not only destroyed, but that the spoils of war were far beyond what they ever expected! God did the same for the children of Israel as they were being set free from their captivity in Egypt. Scripture says the Egyptians loaded them up with articles of gold, silver, and clothing after the Lord secured their freedom from slavery. Through the process of obeying God in the warfare, *God gave them much more than was in the original promise.* He not only secured the boundaries He had set for them, but caused them to gain wealth in the process.

As the Lord brings us into victory, we need to ask Him what spoils of war He has for us to gather. What has the enemy been holding from us that he must now give up as a result of our victory? In some cases it may be literal wealth. In other cases it may be salvation for our loved ones. It could be restoration of destroyed relationships. It could be a physical healing or deliverance from what has been tormenting us. No matter what spoils of war God has for us, we need to understand that the very nature of war is that the one who is defeated must relinquish something to the victor. Be sure that you have gathered all the spoils that the Lord has for you when you come into victory.

In addition to the wealth they gathered, the army of Judah was strengthened for future battles as they were able to gather the swords, shields, and other weapons of war from their fallen enemies. This represents a new strength and a new anointing that comes in victory. As we gain each victory in the war over prophetic fulfillment, God releases a new anointing of authority on us that gives us even greater power to overthrow our enemy in the battles that lie ahead.

A Time to War and a Time to Rest

Ecclesiastes 3:1,8 says, "To everything there is a season, a time for every purpose under heaven.... A time for war!" When it is a time for war, we must have a paradigm for war! The church is being prepared to enter its most dynamic season of warfare, worship, and harvest. When it is a time for war—WAR! David's greatest downfall came during his reign, when it was time to go to war and he stayed home. Passivity in a time of war is disastrous.

There are also times of rest. Not every season of our lives is meant to be marked by warfare. There is a time for everything, including rest. In fact, without seasons of rest, we will never be able to quiet our hearts long enough to hear the voice of the Lord, or to gain revelation for how we should move forward. We need to be wise about how the Lord intends to bring prophetic fulfillment into our lives.

Yes, there will be times of war when we need to stand up and fight. However, the enemy will attempt to prolong our seasons of warfare in order to rob us of our strength. God's grace covers our natural lack of strength during seasons of war. But when God is ready to move us on, we are no longer covered by the same measure of grace. We must never get so caught up in our warfare that we take our eyes off of the Lord, and that we do not enter into the rest He has for us so that we can continue moving forward.

Notes

[1] Some of the material in this section has been adapted from Chuck D. Pierce and Rebecca Wagner Sytsema, *Receiving the Word of the Lord* (Colorado Springs, CO: Wagner Publications, 1999), pp. 24-25.
[2] Graham Cooke, *Developing Your Prophetic Gifting* (Kent, England: Sovereign World, Ltd., 1994), p. 119.
[3] Ibid., p. 120.
[4] Ibid., p 123.
[5] Cindy Jacobs, *The Voice of God* (Ventura, CA: Regal Books, 1995), p. 85.
[6] Jim W. Goll, *Kneeling on the Promises* (Grand Rapids, MI: Chosen Books, 1999), p. 172.
[7] Ibid., p. 173.
[8] Chuck D. Pierce and Rebecca Wagner Sytsema, *Possessing Your Inheritance* (Ventura, CA: Renew, 1999), pp. 134-135.
[9] Ibid., p. 23.
[10] Goll, p. 173.
[11] Cindy Jacobs, *Possessing the Gates of the Enemy* (Tarrytown, NY: Chosen Books, 1991), p. 178.

CHAPTER FOUR

Hope
Deferred

So shall My word be that goes forth from My mouth;
it shall not return to Me void, but it shall accomplish
what I please, and it shall prosper in the thing for
which I sent it (Isa. 55:11).

Have you ever had a promise from God that you kept expecting to be fulfilled, but nothing ever happened? Have you had a desire that you felt God put in your heart that never materialized? Did you once have faith to see the plan of God for your life manifest, but now that faith seems dry and distant? Did you have *great expectations* for God moving on your behalf, but are still waiting?

Now we come to what is perhaps the most difficult aspect of prophetic fulfillment: hope deferred. When our hope is deferred, we can experience it in one of two ways. It can be either a promise that seems as though it will never be fulfilled, or it can be a promise fulfilled, but the fruit of that promise is dead. Have you ever experienced the death of a promise? It can truly cause the heart to become sick (see Prov. 13:12a).

Another Day of Prophetic Fulfillment

We began this book by telling the story of my daughter, Rebekah's birth and what a great day of prophetic fulfillment that was. If you will recall, however, my wife, Pam, knew that the barrenness in her life would break off because in 1980 the Lord had promised that she would bear twins. As the barrenness broke, she gave birth to our beautiful daughter, Rebekah, followed by our son John Mark. Then in 1987 she became pregnant again. We noticed that she was getting larger more quickly than she had with the first two pregnancies. We learned it was because she indeed was carrying twins! What God had promised was now in motion.

She carried the babies to term and, on February 6, 1988, Pam gave birth to two beautiful identical twin boys whom we named Jesse David and Jacob Levi. God's promise was fulfilled! But something was wrong in their new little bodies. One baby had a serious heart problem, and the other had a serious liver problem. Within one week of their birth, both of our new sons had died. I watched as they were born, and I held them as they died. The grief and mourning was almost overwhelming. The promise of these twins was the reason we could believe that the barrenness in our lives would be broken, and now, just as it was being fulfilled, that promise had died.

My coauthor, Rebecca Sytsema, had a similar experience. Shortly after she and her husband, Jack, were married, they inquired of the Lord as to the timing of having children. They received a clear prophetic word from a highly respected prophet that the time had come. They confirmed the word, and shortly thereafter conceived their first child. Within a few weeks of her due date, however, their baby daughter, Anna Jean, died in Rebecca's womb without warning or explanation. Their promise was stillborn.

How could this be? How could the Lord speak His promise so clearly only to allow it to die?

Submitting to the Hand of God

When the second of our twins died, we had an outdoor memorial service for him. During that service, Pam stood up and sang a beautiful song out over the field. It was an incredible moment. One week after the death of the second baby a friend called and said they had a real problem with the fact that the children died. First of all, they had a problem with God allowing their deaths. Second, they were also having a problem with how Pam was dealing with this trauma with seemingly unshakable faith.

Pam told our friend, "If there's one thing I've learned in my life, it's that the quicker I submit to the hand of God, the quicker I can resist the devil. I have chosen to submit to God's hand in this circumstance. And in submitting to the hand of God, He will give me the ability to overcome the enemy so that the double portion that has been robbed will be returned."

The Lord was speaking through my beautiful wife. Those words went deeply into my spirit and I have carried them since that time. Even when we don't understand what has happened in our lives, in the midst of our loss and resulting grief we need to learn to submit quickly to God's greater plan for our lives. If we will always submit our lives to God, those incredibly hard things that we go through will truly become some sort of blessing in the hand of the Lord, and they will produce a greater prophetic fulfillment in our life.

Another Promise Fulfilled

In my case, the Lord turned the circumstances of the twins' deaths into a tremendous restoration for my whole family. My extended family, still distant in our relationships because of the crisis we had lived through, now rallied and bonded together in this new trauma. The Lord had spoken to me when I was 18 and had given me a promise. That promise was: "I will restore all that you have lost." These words had been the driving force of my life since that time.

There is a certain level of joy we would never come to know if we had not experienced loss. The deeper the sorrow, the more capacity for joy we seem to have.

Now in this terrible loss and trauma that Pam and I were experiencing, I was actually watching Him restore our family unit which had been so fragmented. My sister and I, who had struggled in our relationship, now were bonding. My mother, instead of being bitter and hardened as in the past, was now comforting us and walking with us through it all. An estranged uncle, whom I had not heard from since I was 16, called and responded. At 35 years of age, I was seeing God fulfill the promise I had been walking in since I was 18. The death of one promise was the catalyst for bringing life and fulfillment to another. That is God's way. What happened in my family as a result of our twins was a true miracle!

Loss Has Benefits

We should allow God to work our situation for good and respond to His love no matter how difficult our circumstance may be. Pam and I both were able to recognize that even in this trauma we were living in of the loss of two children, God was working out a higher level promise of restoration on our behalf. Loss can produce a great acknowledgement of God within you if you will submit to His hand. There are other benefits as well:

Loss produces shaking. During times of loss, God begins to shake us. He removes legalism, fear, condemnation, false expectations, and erroneous thinking about Himself. If you can endure the shaking, you come out in a much stronger place, which results in greater maturity. In the midst of loss, we have a unique opportunity to rise to new levels, and to come to a deeper understanding of God's awesome grace. His grace is always sufficient.

Loss produces joy. There are many Scriptures that link loss to joy. Stop and read Psalm 30. In fact, we put one such passage on the headstone of the twins' grave: "Therefore you now have sorrow; but I will see you again and your heart will rejoice, and your joy no one will take from you" (John 16:22). There is a certain level of joy we would never come to know if we had not experienced loss. The deeper the sorrow, the more capacity for joy we seem to have.

Loss produces change. After experiencing loss, nothing seems the same. Gerald Sittser, who lost his mother, wife, and young daughter in a tragic car accident, writes: "The experience of loss does not have to leave us with the memory of a painful event that stands alone, like a towering monument that dominates the landscape of our lives. Loss can also leave us with the memory of a wonderful story. It can function as a catalyst that pushes us in a new direction, like a closed road that forces us to turn around and find another way to our destination. Who knows what we will discover and see along the way?"[1]

Loss produces resurrection. In *Possessing Your Inheritance*, we write, "We can be assured that when we experience loss, especially of something that was part of our inheritance, God invariably has a plan for restoring it to us. When death comes, for example, God always longs to start a resurrection process. David W. Wiersby, in his book *Gone But Not Lost*, which was written to those grieving the death of a child, writes, 'God's response to death is always life. That doesn't mean he gives another child when one dies. It means that out of the sorrow and ruin of your 'other' life, God gives you a new life.' The same is true for any loss. God's response to loss is always restoration in some form."[2]

When Expectations are Gone, Self-Pity Remains!

When we are in very difficult situations we can easily lose sight of God's promise. This is how we get off target in seeing God fulfill our prophetic destiny. Even though the body of Christ goes through great times of testing, we are not to grow fearful and discouraged. During our testing periods, the enemy takes advantage with a strategy to discourage us. *Discouragement breeds "hope deferred" which* makes the heart sick. When we have a measure of hopelessness within us, we lose our expectation of God.

Future and expectation are synonymous. Our future is linked with an expectation of God moving. This is a time for the church to have its expectation level renewed and raised to another level. Isaiah 59 and 60 is a wonderful prayer guide for you to see this happen in your life. Hope must transcend and move into faith. Faith produces overcoming. Overcoming leads to a demonstration of God's power and a manifestation of His promises.

The Cycle of Self-Pity

Prophecy unlocks your future. Once we get wounded or experience loss, we can lose sight of our future. The biggest demonic force we have to contend with seems to be self-pity. This stops us from seeing God's glory manifest in our life. Self-pity is a demonic force that draws attention to our loss. Instead of our loss directing us to God's continued perfect plan for our life, Self rises up and says: "Pity me for what I have lost." Any time we experience loss, trauma, wounding, or injustice, our mindset can go in two directions. We can live with a belief system that God can heal and forgive. Or our mindset can form rejection, self-defense, and self-pity.

During loss and wounding, we have a tendency to accuse God for the trauma we are experiencing. The power of this accusation leads to a type of fatherlessness. Instead of experiencing the spirit of adoption, we feel abandoned and lost. From our self-defense we actually form a rebellion to authority. We also become unteachable. We have a mindset that says, "No one understands me or what I am going through." The Johan complex overtakes us.

We also begin to think there is no solution to our problem. We wake up thinking, "There is no way out." We fall into apathy because we have no hope of healing or restoration. We know we should be living a godly life; therefore, religious mechanisms become a solace to us. We even gain a martyr complex and may say, "O woe is me. This is my cross to bear. Look how heavy is my cross." This type of thinking leads us to not fight when we need to. Instead of fighting and advancing, we become a slave to comfort and the status quo.

We forget that we are called to fellowship with His sufferings. This type of fellowship leads us to His resurrection power manifesting in us. If we ever lose sight of the love of God, we turn to self. God's love forces us to deal with the thoughts that are listed above. I have experienced enough freedom in my own life to know when I am not free. Faith works by love. Once we experience His liberty and love, we will be able to resist that call from Self to be pitied and can overthrow hope deferred.

Joseph: A Picture of Resisting and Overcoming Hope Deferred

I love to teach on Joseph. His is one of my favorite stories in the Bible. Through Joseph, we see how faith gives us the ability to see our losses come back to us in an increased and restored form.

When we first read of Joseph, we see a young man with incredible favor and many prophetic promises. He shared his promises and revelations freely, perhaps too freely. Throughout his life, the garments that he wore were symbols of the favor that God had graced his life with. The famous "coat of many colors" represented both favor and a double-portion anointing from his father. But his garment was not secure. Even though this was the will of God for his life, there were many trials and losses he would face before entering into his prophetic destiny.

The Betrayal of Brothers

In their jealousy over Joseph's favor, his brothers became enraged and literally tore Joseph's garment off. Joseph was betrayed by his brothers and his favor was stripped from him. He was sold into slavery and it was reported to his father that he was dead. Betrayals that we experience in our lives are linked with covenant breaking. This is one heartbreaking form of hope deferred. When we have been betrayed, a covenant of some type has generally been breached, which can cause us to fall into distrust and hopelessness.

Divorce is, perhaps, the most prominent form of covenant breaking. It is often said that the true victims of divorce are the children of the marriage. The fruit of the covenant is what the enemy targets when covenants are broken. He attempts to use these kinds of events in our lives to not only strip our favor from us, but to cause God's plan for the generations to follow to become derailed through dysfunctional relationships and distrust in God. But God can transcend these events and reposition us for prophetic fulfillment. Again it is a matter of submitting to the hand of God.

We have to ask ourselves, have past betrayals stopped us from having favor today? The moment those betrayals stop you, you can lose favor just because of your own bitterness. But, as Joseph submitted to the Lord in the midst of the betrayal of his brothers, the Lord once again brought him into new favor with his master (see Gen. 39:4). He had so much favor, in fact, that the master made Joseph his overseer and put all that he had under Joseph's control. God has ways, even in the midst of slavery, to bring favor and put us in strategic positions.

False Accusations

In the midst of Joseph's new position of favor, however, we see that he suffers further loss through false accusation. Here his master's wife becomes angry with Joseph when he refuses to have an affair with her. During the encounter, as Joseph tries to flee the situation, she grabs hold of his garment and rips it off his body. She then uses the garment as false evidence to accuse Joseph of trying to rape her. Once again Joseph is left naked, without favor, and in shame.

False accusations can bring unwarranted shame and reproach on our lives, causing us to lose favor. That is why the devil loves to set up false accusations against us. We must remember, however, that true humility does not receive false accusation. If we are not guilty of the accusation, sometimes God will require us to set the record straight and not just take it and think ourselves to be humble and somehow more spiritual. That is nothing more than a false sense of humility which is a counterfeit of God's intentions. We may have to go into a hard prison over it for a season, but if we've been falsely accused, sooner or later God will set that record straight in our lives and get us back on track.

Lessons From Prison

After Joseph was falsely accused, he was sent to prison where he seemed forgotten and abandoned. He had been rejected over and over, and was now left to die in disgrace. Prophetic fulfillment seemed very unlikely by this point. The future, if there was one, seemed quite dim. Yet in the midst of all these adversities, did Joseph allow his circumstances to stop him from moving into a new dimension of favor? No. Genesis 39:21 says that the Lord showed mercy on him and gave him favor in the sight of the keeper of the prison.

We must not let fear remove our favor. We must not let grief remove our favor. We must not let betrayal or false accusations or imprisonment or unfair circumstances or rejection remove our favor. Even though Joseph was stripped, he continued submitting to the hand of God so that He could clothe him once again.

Furthermore we see that Joseph kept his gifts working. Often when we fall into self-pity and somewhere in the process we stop allowing our gifts to work. But when Joseph was in prison he allowed the Lord to continue working through him by interpreting dreams. In the midst of adversity and hope deferred Joseph did not stop moving forward in the plan of God for his life. As a result,

God found the perfect time to bring Joseph out of the prison, and once again clothed him with favor: "Then Pharaoh sent and called Joseph, and they brought him quickly out of the dungeon; and he shaved, changed his clothing, and came to Pharaoh" (Gen. 41:14).

The Best is Yet Ahead!

Just as God moved on the heart of Pharaoh on behalf of Joseph, He can move on anybody on your behalf. Some of you may be waiting for a mate or for a promotion or for promises for your children. For these things to occur, God is going to have to move on somebody on your behalf. We need to have confidence in God.

One of the most faith-building phrases in the Bible is "But God…" It is in these amazing words that we find hope for what lies ahead:

"My flesh and my heart fail; *but God* is the strength of my heart and my portion forever" (Ps. 73:26, italics added).

"The nations will rush like the rushing of many waters; *but God* will rebuke them and they will flee far away, and be chased like the chaff of the mountains before the wind, like a rolling thing before the whirlwind" (Isa. 17:13, italics added).

"For indeed he was sick almost unto death; *but God* had mercy on him, and not only on him but on me also, lest I should have sorrow upon sorrow" (Phil. 2:27, italics added).

"*But God* demonstrates His own love toward us, in that while we were still sinners, Christ died for us" (Rom. 5:8, italics added).

Joseph knew that *But God* had been at work in his life. He said in Genesis 45:8, "So now it was not you who sent me here, *but God*; and He has made me a father to Pharaoh, and lord of all his house, and a ruler throughout all the land of Egypt." And again in Genesis 50:20 he said, "But as for you, you meant evil against me; *but God* meant it for good, in order to bring it about as it is this day, to save many people alive."

Joseph knew that it was *But God* who allowed him to be betrayed, to go through false accusation, to be abandoned, to be rejected, to be imprisoned and forgotten. It was *But God* that stripped him of his favor time and again. Yet in each instance, it was *But God* that showed him mercy and reclothed him in favor. It was *But God* that brought about the prophetic fulfillment and destiny that was meant to be Joseph's portion. For it was through this rejected, abandoned, accused prisoner that God saved the entire region from a devastating famine. Through Joseph, the promises that God made to Abraham concerning his family line were saved and restored, which we will discuss more in the next chapter.

Once you understand that, regardless of your circumstances and regardless of what you have been through that has caused your hope to be deferred and your heart to become sick, *But God* is still well able to fulfill the promises He has for you. Once you embrace *But God* in your heart of hearts, you won't get bogged down under that self-pity and defeat, but will instead be able to say, "*But God* is at work in my life! I will not allow favor to be stripped from me, I will keep operating in the gifts He has given me, and I will move forward into my destiny because *But God* will make a way!" For those who are able to allow this kind of faith in God to arise, it is without a doubt that the best is yet ahead!

Casting Off Our Old Garments

Just as the clothing that Joseph wore signified His favor, in the same way the spiritual garment that we are wearing represents where we are. Our garment may be made up of the pain of losses and hope deferred. We may be wearing a spirit of heaviness, as described in Isaiah 61. *But God* sent His son, "To console those who mourn in Zion, to give them beauty for ashes, the oil of joy for mourning, the garment of praise for the spirit of heaviness; that they may be called trees of righteousness, the planting of the LORD, that He may be glorified" (Isa. 61:3).

It doesn't matter what the enemy has done to distort your identity in God. You can shake the remnants of those tattered garments off and be reclothed! After the loss of our twins, the doctors warned us not to have any more children as they too might be born with the same defects. *But God* did not agree. Since that time we have had two more beautiful, healthy boys. I can't say that it was all easy, especially the first year after that loss. *But God* has shown Himself faithful. He has restored. He has healed. He has moved us forward to new levels of prophetic fulfillment, and continues us on an incredible journey of faith and joy.

Loss is simply a painful fact of life. Yet as we submit to the hand of *But God*, it can become a tool that propels us from a season of loss into a *now* season of joyous prophetic fulfillment.

Declare each of the following over your life and allow your expectation of *But God* to be renewed:

- ◆ Expect the Lord to raise up a standard against your foes (Isa. 59:19)!
- ◆ Expect your spirit to arise with glory so that oppression and depression break off of you (Isa. 60:1)!
- ◆ Expect the Lord's presence to rest on you (Isa. 60:2)!
- ◆ Expect new vision to arise within you (Isa. 60:4)!
- ◆ Expect new joy to overwhelm you (Isa. 60:5)!
- ◆ Expect that the "camels are coming" to your house with new supply (Isa. 60:6-7)!
- ◆ Expect praise to begin to cover your region, breaking the power of desolation (Isa. 60:6)!
- ◆ Expect God to release the strength and supply to complete your building project (Isa. 60:9-10)!

♦ Expect new favor to come upon you, and new doors and connections to open for you (Isa. 60:10)!

♦ Expect the spirit of poverty that has been holding your gates shut to let go, and expect the gate of provision to come open and stay open (Isa. 60:11)!

Notes

[1] Gerald L. Sittser, *A Grace Disguised* (Grand Rapids, MI: Zondervan Publishing, 1996), p. 130.

[2] Chuck D. Pierce and Rebecca Wagner Sytsema, *Possessing Your Inheritance* (Ventura, CA: Renew Books, 1999), pp. 74-75.

CHAPTER FIVE

Your Land Shall Rejoice:
Prophetic Fulfillment in Generations and Territories

But when the time of the promise drew near which God had sworn to Abraham, the people grew and multiplied in Egypt (Acts 7:17).

Joel 2:21-29 says, "Fear not, O land; be glad and rejoice, for the Lord has done marvelous things.... For the open pastures are springing up, and the tree bears its fruit; the fig tree and the vine yield their strength. Be glad then, you children of Zion, and rejoice in the Lord your God; for He has given you the former rain faithfully, and He will cause the rain to come down for you–the former rain, and the latter rain in the first month. The threshing floors shall be full of wheat and the vats shall overflow with new wine and oil. So I will restore to you the years that the swarming locust has eaten, the crawling locust, the consuming locust, and the chewing locust, My great army which I sent among you.... And it shall come to pass afterward that I will pour out My Spirit on all flesh; your sons and your daughters shall prophesy, your old men shall dream dreams, your young men shall see visions. And also on my menservants and on my maidservants I will pour out My Spirit in those days." This prophecy from Joel, reveals the heart of God to restore and bless His people.

God's Plan Can Be Deferred

In the last chapter we talked about how our hope can be deferred. But did you ever stop to think about how God's plan can also be deferred? He may have plans and destiny for us that we, through choices, disobedience, sin, misdirection, or other circumstances, never fulfill. When God sets the destiny for our lives, it is not just for our own benefit. Many others, even whole territories, are meant to benefit from the Holy Spirit's work through us. Therefore, whenever we do not allow the Holy Spirit to carry out the work He intended to do through us, He has to look for someone who will. That is when God's plan is deferred—not only for us as individuals, but for what He was trying to accomplish in our family, our circle of influence, and our territory. However, this does not stop God from moving.

Joel was prophesying at a time of great devastation to the entire land of Judah. He was prophesying that there would come a "Church Age," a time when all people would call on the name of the Lord, be saved from their sins and understand God's Kingdom purposes in the earth realm. The people of Judah had abandoned God's purposes. However, the prophet began to see a time in the future when the Spirit of God would be poured out. Every person, young and old alike, men and women, slave and free, all individuals would receive the opportunity to experience the Spirit of God. Of course we find the account of this prophecy being fulfilled in Acts 2.

Four Dimensions of Restorative Prophecy

What's the real issue here? First of all, even when we stray from God's purpose He already has a plan in place for redemption. I call this restorative prophecy. God is working in four dimensions. We see this in the prophecy from Joel:

1. He is working to restore our lives *personally* — (I will restore to you).
2. He is working *corporately* — (be glad then you children of Zion).
3. He is working *territorially* — (fear not, o land).
4. He is working *generationally* — (your sons and daughters shall…).

Prophetic fulfillment is intricate. When God is speaking into our life and has a destiny for us individually, that destiny also affects the corporate vision where we are a part, the territory or land wherein we live or are assigned to, and the generations to come. The contrary to this is when we don't fulfill the plan of God for our life, that lack of fulfillment affects the rest of the body of Christ that our gift was intended to be aligned with, the city and nation of which we are a part or were assigned to, and the generations to come.

Waiting for the Next Generation

In Chapter One I told of the great potential my father had while he was alive. The choices he made, however, caused him to miss his destiny. The only legacy he was able to leave was not what he accomplished through his own obedience to God, but the hope that his children might accomplish their destinies.

To illustrate this, we can think of dogs. Let's suppose, for example, that a dog is bred for the purpose of becoming a seeing-eye dog. She may come from the best line of seeing-eye dogs, may have the correct temperament, and may even show great potential early on. But, if the dog refuses to allow herself to submit to the rigorous training process, all the breeding and potential in the world does not change the fact that she will never become a seeing-eye dog. She may become a good companion dog and lead a life of comfort, but she will never accomplish what she could have if only she had allowed herself to be trained. Her usefulness as a seeing-eye dog lies only in the generation she breeds in hopes that her pups may be able to do what she herself would not allow.

God's Plan for Generations

Just as God has a plan for our lives as individuals, He also has plans for entire bloodlines that are passed on from generation to generation. In our individualistic society, it may be a little hard to grasp, but just as surely as our physical DNA ties in to our families, our spiritual DNA is also inherited. The pages of genealogies in the Bible are there for a reason. The family line from which someone came was as important as who they were. Why? It is because the promises and anointings of God are often passed down through families.

God's Covenant with Families

Over and over we read of God as the God of Abraham, Isaac, and Jacob. It was from this line that the Jewish nation, God's chosen people, came into being. It was the result of a covenant. Many of the covenants God made dealt with families:

♦ **Noahic Covenant.** After the Flood, God made a covenant with Noah and his family: "Then God spoke to Noah and to his sons with him, saying: 'And as for Me, behold, I establish My covenant with you and with your descendants after you,'" (Gen. 9:8-9). Through this family God established a new beginning for the human race.

♦ **Abrahamic Covenant.** As we have already mentioned, God's covenant with Abraham had very specific familial promises. In fact, Abraham, Isaac, and Jacob, as the three fathers of the nation of Israel, were all partakers of the same covenant. As part of the covenant, God promised that through this family, all the families of the earth would be blessed (Gen. 12:3).

♦ **Davidic Covenant.** The covenant God made with David after the death of Saul established David's kingship. God promised David that his seed would rule over his kingdom forever. It was, of course, into David's family line that Jesus was eventually born.

♦ **The New Covenant.** Through The New Covenant, all those who partake of the salvation of Christ are adopted into the family of God, with Jesus as the firstborn, and a vast family of brothers and sisters. It is through His own family that all God's work on earth is carried out. He perfects His family bloodline. We find in Romans 9:11 that He grafts us back into the Abrahamic blessing so that He can accomplish all in His people that has not yet been accomplished. Thank God for this spirit of adoption (Romans 8).

Family lines are indeed important to God. The family of which you are a part, whether by blood or through adoption, has both a godly inheritance and an evil inheritance that Satan has used to try to pervert God's plans, which we discuss in great detail in our book *Possessing Your Inheritance* (Renew). Prophetic fulfillment, therefore, cannot just be looked at individually, but must also be viewed from a familial perspective.

Preserving Life

In the last chapter we talked a great deal about Joseph and the prophetic fulfillment in his own life. But what did Joseph's obedience mean for his family and their prophetic fulfillment? Joseph was reconnected with his family in the midst of a great famine. Joseph, having been forewarned by God, was put in a place of authority to be sure that provisions were made for surviving the famine. As he discussed this with his brothers, he said, "But now, do not therefore be grieved nor angry with yourselves because you sold me here; for

God is always looking for how He will connect His promises from one generation to another generation... Even those prodigals who seem so far from God's plan for their lives always have some opportunity to return to God's plan for them.

God sent me before you to preserve life... And God sent me before you to preserve a posterity for you in the earth, and to save your lives by a great deliverance" (Gen. 45:5,7).

I love the fact that Joseph realized his fulfilled vision even in all his trials and testings. Joseph was faithful to the vision and dream God had given him. His life proves that vision restrains people from sin. Proverbs 29:18 says this, "Where there is no revelation, the people cast off restraint." That means that without restraint of prophetic revelation or insight, a people stray from the path that God had intended for them, go backwards, and finally disintegrate.

God worked it out so that Joseph would be in a position to preserve the life of his family; the family to which God had made the Abrahamic Covenant. Preserving life is actually revival. It is taking what has once been alive and thriving, and breathing new life into it.

There will always be an awakening in God's people or in your life to preserve what God is trying to do in your family. We can be assured that prophetic fulfillment will come, because once there has been a promise made in your bloodline, God will activate it at some point to preserve that promise to bring it into fullness. Even if you are the first one in your bloodline to be saved, when God created that bloodline He had a destiny for it. Now He is awakening that destiny through you. As in Joseph's case, it doesn't matter what you've been through. God is at work with preserving life to bring His purposes about in your family.

Prophetic Fulfillment: Generation to Generation

In order to help us more fully understand how prophetic fulfillment works from generation to generation, let's take a look at Abraham and see the six steps it took to pass the covenant promises onto Isaac so that Isaac could come into his prophetic fulfillment.

1. A persevering faith.

Abraham had a covenant promise for his family, which included a son being born to him from his aging wife, Sarah. Abraham had to stand and believe God for his promise as the years of natural fertility dwindled and passed. Even so he maintained a persevering faith, and the promise through which the covenant would be passed was finally born when Isaac arrived.

As we have said before, God has a destiny for every bloodline and we need to come into agreement with what God is trying to do, even if we don't know the specifics of how it will work out. It requires a persevering faith that often overlooks the natural circumstances in favor of *But God!* As we allow that faith to arise within us, we will see the covenant promises of God over ourselves and our families begin to take shape as God causes the circumstances of our lives to come into alignment with His promise to us. We see other individuals in the Bible that are great examples for us concerning persevering faith. Daniel withstood the lions, Caleb in his 80s advanced into his promise, Sarah in her 90s conceived. What wonderful examples of faith.

2. The covenant promise will always be tested.

In Genesis 22 we see that Abraham underwent a strong test. Here God calls Abraham to take his precious son, Isaac, and lay him on an alter in sacrifice. It must have taken a tremendous level of obedience on Abraham's part to make that choice and lay his son down to die. But Abraham understood that this was God's directive. He knew that somewhere in the midst of his obedience to God, God would have to settle the outcome and fulfill His covenant. The obedience was up to Abraham, and the rest was God's problem. Of course we know that in the end Abraham was not required to follow through and kill Isaac, but even if he had, God would have had to find another way to fulfill His covenant.

The testing of our promises is an inevitable step in prophetic fulfillment. In fact, if we don't get past that step, our promises will not be fulfilled, either for ourselves or for our families. Like Abraham, we need to understand that our role is obedience to God, and the rest is up to Him. Period.

3. Testing unveils provision.

Once Abraham passed the test, provision came. There in a thicket was a ram caught by its horns. Abraham was able to take the ram and offer it as a sacrifice to the Lord instead of offering Isaac. In fact, Abraham named that place "The Lord Will Provide" (Gen. 22:14) as a testimony to God supplying what was needed. As we pass the testing of our promises, God will reveal hidden provision for moving us forward. Things that we were not able to see before will become evident to us, and we will gain new strategy for continuing to move toward God's plan for us.

4. Promises extend to new generations.

Another result of Abraham passing the test was that God extended a new promise to him for the generations of his family to come. God said to him, "By Myself I have sworn, says the LORD, because you have done this thing, and have not withheld your son, your only son—blessing I will bless you, and in multiplying I will multiply your descendants as the stars of the heaven and as the sand which is on the seashore; and your descendants shall possess the gate of their enemies. In your seed all the nations of the earth shall be blessed, because you have obeyed My voice" (Gen. 22:16-18).

God is always looking for how He will connect His promises from one generation to another generation. We must acknowledge the generations and see that God has promises for the generations to come. Even those prodigals who seem so far from God's plan for their lives always have some opportunity to return to God's plan for them.

5. Connecting to pass the mantle.

Many times we must participate in supernatural connecting so the next generation receives the blessing from the previous generation and continues progressing in that blessing. Years later, Abraham had come to an awakening that the promise that he had been given, which had been extended to Isaac, could not be completed if Isaac had no wife with whom he could have children of his own. Abraham, therefore, instructed his servant to find just the right wife for Isaac. Through Abraham's careful instructions, the servant found Rebekah, who became Isaac's wife.

What is it that we are to provide the next generation for them to move on in God's covenant promise for them? Certainly a godly upbringing (Proverbs 22:6 says, "Train up a child in the way he should go, and when he is old he will not depart from it."), an understanding of who they are in Christ, and lots of prayer top the list. But beyond good parenting, we need to gain instruction from the Lord regarding our role in assisting the next generation reach prophetic fulfillment in their lives.

6. Conception for the future.

Isaac gaining a wife was not enough to ensure that God's promise would carry on. He and Rebekah had to conceive the next generation. There has to be a conception in order to bring forth the prophetic fulfillment. We must not stop until we are sure that we have conceived and brought to birth all that God asks of us.

God's covenant promise to Abraham also required obedience for prophetic fulfillment. Abraham was required to go through all these steps and partner with God in faith and obedience, even in the face of years of discouragement. Yet through Abraham's faithfulness, all the families of the earth truly have been blessed. What is it that God longs to accomplish through your family line, and what role do you play in your family's prophetic fulfillment?

The Issue of Territory

There is another issue to be considered as we discuss prophetic fulfillment — God's destiny for a *territory*. A few years back Bob Beckett brought a tremendous teaching on territories. In his book, *Commitment to Conquer*, he writes, "The human race is not the only object of God's affection. We are indeed the primary objects of His love here on earth, but not the exclusive recipients…God also loves the land He has created. He cares about actual, physical soil and what comes forth from that soil...Since the time of Adam, God has been busy distributing the peoples of the earth throughout the continents and islands He fashioned as their dwelling places. Indeed, He created every nation, province, territory and city for His own purposes."[1]

In fact, before God made any covenants with families, He made the Edenic Covenant with Adam. In this first interaction God had with man, He commanded Adam to do several things concerning the land. He was to subdue the earth, to take dominion of it, and to till the ground—he was to tend the Garden (Gen. 2:15).

Places are very important in the Bible. Bob Beckett goes on to write, "While the Bible mentions missions 12 times, borders and coasts are mentioned 96 times. Justification by faith is cited 70 times, while countries and nations are referred to 180 times. The virgin birth appears twice, while regions are mentioned 15 times. Repentance is noted 110 times, while the earth is referenced 908 times. Baptism appears 80 times, while ground appears 188 times. Christ's return is mentioned 318 times, while land totals 1,717 times."[2]

Planted in the Right Place

Why are places so important? Because God has a destiny for individuals and families, the place that they live also has a destiny. In fact, the two are so closely linked that often we will not fulfill our destiny unless we are positioned in the right territory. And, without the right people in a territory, it will not fulfill its destiny.

Jeremiah 32:41 says, "I will rejoice over them to do them good, and I will assuredly *plant* them in this land, with all My heart and with all My soul" (italics added). God very carefully places us where we are to be. One of my favorite exhortations from Bob Beckett's book says, "Even if there is somewhere else you long to be, ask yourself two questions:

"*Who put you where you are?*

"*Why are you there?*

"There can by only two answers to these questions: obedience or rebellion. You are in a place either because God put you there or because you put yourself there... If you are there out of rebellion, I have a word for you: Move, as fast as you can! Find out where God wants you and get there. Even if it feels as if you are being led out of Jerusalem into Babylon, remember that the Lord sees far beyond what you or I can see in our lives. Obedience to God always brings ultimate peace.

"If you know God has placed you where you are, even if it seems like Babylon, I have a word for you: Stay there as long as God asks."[3]

This is a very important principle for us to understand. Our destiny cannot be separated from the destiny of the territory we are called to. Acts 17:26 says that God predetermines the places we are to seek Him. When we are in that place, we are positioned to gain the strategy necessary to secure our portion.

Prophetic Fulfillment for Territories

As we have already mentioned, it is not only for our benefit that we must be planted in the right place. The more a territory can come into its destiny, the more light of God's Spirit can be found in that place. The brighter God's glorious light shines, the more of Satan's darkness is dispelled. In such an atmosphere we see greater levels of God's will being done, including souls being saved, people walking in their full giftings, and a general improvement in the quality of life. That is why spiritual warfare over territories is such an intense battle. Satan is dealt a great blow when territorial victories are won.

Apostolic Alignment is Necessary for Prophetic Fulfillment

God has a perfect governmental structure to produce transformation in the earth realm. He has a perfect order in His government that cannot be resisted by the desolation of our land. Lands go into desolation when people transgress, sin, fall into idolatry, and deviate from God's ultimate plan. Once this deviation occurs, demonic forces have the right to establish themselves in the land and hold territories captive. There are four main categories of defilement of the land: covenant breaking, idolatry, immorality, and unjust bloodshed. When Joel was talking about the locust entering the land of Judah and devouring both land and people, these defilements had all occurred.

However, we find that God has a perfect order in His Kingdom to break defilement and bring prophetic fulfillment. When Jesus was ascending into heaven, Ephesians 4:11 says He "gave gifts" to humankind. In 1 Corinthians 12, Paul shows how each member has an individual relationship with the Lord, but we are corporately dependent upon each other. In other words, we can't fully come into our prophetic destiny unless we align our gift properly with other members of the body. He then sets an order of alignment in verse 28: "First apostles, second prophets, third teachers, after that miracles, then gifts of healings, helps, administration, varieties of tongues."

Our gift must work within the order that God has prescribed. Therefore, "second prophets" must align their prophetic revelation with "first apostles." This will produce prophetic fulfillment. The word "first" means prototype or model. Therefore, what God is saying, prophesying, or promising to us individually, corporately, territorially, and generationally can only be modeled properly in this alignment. When our promises are aligned properly in God's divine governmental order, we will see the Harvest of the promises in the field where we are planted.

Capernaum:
A Biblical Analysis of Territorial Transformation

I have gone through and analyzed the cities that Jesus visited. First of all, we see a pattern in the Word of God that He had a perfect time to visit each city. The people of that city then had the choice of recognizing Him and receiving His teaching and authority, or rejecting Him. When Jesus visited a city He not only affected the people but every institute of society within that city. His glory permeated the way they lived. His visitation brought changes to religious, economic, governmental (legal and military), and educational structures.

In Capernaum we see that He first visited the synagogue and taught. Notice He dealt with the way they operated in the religious worship aspect of their society in Capernaum. Mark 1:22 says, "He taught them as one having authority, and not as the scribes." He used a *teaching* gift. This caused a demon, or unclean spirit that had inhabited one of the men in the synagogue, to cry out. Verse 27 says they were all amazed and said, "What is this? What new doctrine is this? For with authority he commands even the unclean spirits, and they obey him!" This caused His fame to go throughout the entire region. This is how transformation works.

We also see Him visiting Capernaum again and *preaching* the Word to them (Mark 2). Notice He uses a different type of gift, and He uses a different method of transformation. He was also in a different setting, meeting in the home of an individual. We then see Him demonstrating a different type of power by forgiving the sins of a paralytic man. The religious reasoning of the time could not accept this as valid, and it completely rattled the scribes. Jesus asked them a question: "Which is easier to say to the paralytic, 'Your sins are forgiven you,' or to say, 'Arise, take up your bed and walk.'" Jesus had the prerogative to choose how He would transform the culture. We find the result of this action that "all were amazed and glorified God."

When Jesus comes to visit our city we must respond. The glory of His visitation will either bring transformation or hardness of heart. In Matthew 11:20,23-24 we find this: "Then he began to rebuke the cities in which most of His mighty work had been done, because they did not repent: '...And you, Capernaum, who are exalted to heaven, will be brought down to Hades; for if the mighty works which were done in you had been done in Sodom, it would have remained until this day. But I say to you that it shall be more tolerable for the land of Sodom in the day of judgment than for you.'" When He comes to your city, receive Him!

Almolonga, Guatemala:
A Modern Day Story of Transformation

In his book, *Revival! It Can Transform Your City*, Peter Wagner tells the story of Almolonga, Guatemala: "In the early 1970s Almolonga was a city of degradation in every way possible. Alcohol reigned, and drunkenness was endemic. Men would drink up their wages and go home to beat their wives and children. On Monday mornings the streets would be lined with drunks laid out like firewood. Sleeping around was expected behavior. Disease flourished, and the extreme poverty of the city had cut medical services to a minimum. Violence ran rampant. Children couldn't go to school. Overcrowded jails forced construction of new ones. Natural disasters seemed to be attracted to Almolonga. The land was barren, crops constantly failed, and food was always scarce. In Almolonga, people were born in misery, lived in misery, and died in misery."[4]

After describing a power encounter that changed the spiritual atmosphere of the city, he goes on to describe the same place today: "God has been so highly glorified and exalted in that city of almost 20,000 that Satan is embarrassed and irate... Some 90 percent of the people of Almolonga are born again. The largest and most prominent buildings throughout the hills surrounding the city are evangelical churches...The city is clean. People are bright and cheerful. Well-dressed children attend school and their families stay intact. Of the city's 34 barrooms, 31 have closed. Disease and sickness, now rare, can be treated with readily available medical help...

"Poverty? It is a thing of the past in Almolonga. The farmers raise world-class vegetables, including cabbages the size of basketballs and carrots as large as a man's forearm... The last jail in Almolonga closed nine years ago because there were no more criminals."[5]

Transformed Territories
Equal Transformed Lives

God longs for that kind of transformation in every territory! I long for that kind of change in my own city! As a territory comes into its destiny, the people of that territory are much more likely to come into theirs. Territorial transformation is a key to personal prophetic fulfillment. Almost every principle we have shared in this book applies just as much to territories as to individual lives. Take a moment to glance through what you have already read in this book, but this time with your city in mind. Remember that the territory God has called you to is linked in some way with your own prophetic fulfillment.

What is God's plan for your city? What is its "personality"?

What prophetic words have been spoken over your territory? Even if you are not called as a pastor or a leader within your city, you are a part of God's plan in that place. That is part of God's prophetic promise to you, and seeing your territory succeed is part of your prophetic fulfillment!

Notes

[1] Bob Beckett, *Commitment to Conquer* (Grand Rapids, MI: Chosen Books, 1997), p. 48.

[2] Ibid., p. 53.

[3] Ibid., p. 65-66.

[4] C. Peter Wagner, *Revival! It Can Transform Your City* (Colorado Springs, CO: Wagner Publications, 1999), pp.54-55.

[5] Ibid., pp. 54, 55, 56.

CHAPTER SIX

Ready and Clothed for the Best Ahead:
A Call to Advance!

I will greatly rejoice in the LORD, my soul shall be joyful
in my God; for He has clothed me with the garments
of salvation, he has covered me with the robe of righteousness,
as a bridegroom decks himself with ornaments, and as a bride
adorns herself with her jewels (Isa. 61:10).

A s we set our sights on the road before us and prepare for
prophetic fulfillment, we need to be ready ourselves and be
properly clothed for the days ahead. We must not allow ourselves
to be so diverted by our circumstances that we miss the Lord's plan
for restoration and prophetic fulfillment.

Don't Get Distracted

I love the story of Jesus visiting the home of Mary and Martha.
Martha welcomed Him into her house. Once He was there, Mary

sat at His feet and listened to His word. Martha was proud of her home and glad to have the Lord visiting. However, she missed the purpose of His visit. He was not there on a social visit, but to release His word to the city of Bethany. Luke 10:40 says, "Martha was distracted with much serving." The word "distracted" in Greek is *perispao*, which means to be encumbered and dragged all around.

Mary, on the other hand, seemed to stay very focused on the highest purpose of the moment. Martha even approached the Lord and said, "Lord, do you not care that my sister has left me to serve alone?" In other words, "Make my sister come drag around in circles with me!" As a matter of fact, she even told the Lord what to do. Jesus answered and said to her, "Martha, Martha, you are worried and troubled about many things. But one thing is needed, and Mary has chosen that good part which will not be taken away from her."

This is a time in history when all of the events around us could get us distracted from the highest purpose of God. We have enough with our daily lives and all the cares of the world placed upon us. In the Greek the word "worry" is *merimnao*. This word means "to divide in parts." The word also suggests a distraction, a preoccupation with things causing anxiety, stress, pressure, and the straying from the focused goal that we are called to accomplish. I love Matthew 6:25-30:

"Therefore I say to you, do not worry about your life, what you will eat or what you will drink; not about your body, what you will put on. Is not life more than food and the body more than ***clothing***? Look at the birds of the air...Are you not of more value than they?...So why do you worry about ***clothing***? Consider the lilies of the field, how they grow: they neither toil nor spin; and yet I say to you that even Solomon in all his glory was not arrayed like one of these. Now if God clothes the grass of the field, which today is, and tomorrow is thrown into the oven, will He not much more ***clothe*** you, O you of little faith" (emphasis added).

Distraction and worry can fragment us. Martha got preoccupied, where Mary got focused. Because of Mary's focus and attention, she was going to be able to perceive the best that was yet ahead for her. Martha's distraction put her in danger of missing the best that God had for her. It wasn't that Martha never worshiped. The fact was that she just got distracted and preoccupied instead of taking the opportunity to gain necessary revelation for her future. We must work when God says work, but we need to be intimate when we have the opportunity to be intimate. Whatever we are doing, we need to stay focused.

Lazarus Come Forth!

Let's follow the story of Mary and Martha's relationship with Jesus. They get into a terrible crisis over their brother's sickness. They ask Jesus to come because they have seen His power in the past. They send a message to Him saying, "Lord, behold, he whom you love is sick." Jesus sends back a reply and says, "This sickness is not unto death, but for the glory of God." This is a wonderful story in John 11. I love the verse 5: "Now Jesus loved Martha and her sister and Lazarus." So many times when we are in a terrible circumstance in our life we seem to forget the Lord's love for us. Other times when we are asking Him to fulfill a desire of our heart and He says, "Wait" we lose sight of His faithfulness to us.

We can learn many things from the story of Lazarus:

1. We should not be coerced out of the Father's timing. Jesus watched for His key *opportune times* to reflect the Father's glory from Heaven. With the Lord's love for Lazarus, Mary, and Martha, it might seem that Jesus would have immediately left His post and went to His sick friend. However, He waited two days. This event

revealed His ability to control His emotion. Even friends and close acquaintances could not coerce Him out of the Father's timing. He was not moved to action by external forces.

This is key for us in days ahead. Our emotions must be intact to keep us in God's perfect timing. This will ensure that we will be at the right place at the right time. In those days the rabbis taught that after three days the soul returned to God. It was believed that the soul hovered near the deceased for three days. Jesus' delay meant Lazarus was in the grave for four days. This meant he was good and dead, and that his soul had departed. This is the only record in the Bible of a resurrection occurring past three days.

2. He chose the key place to address the strongman of unbelief. Bethany was a gateway into Judea, a stronghold of religion and unbelief. Look for those key gateways in the region where you live. Unbelief is such a hindering force that it will keep us from seeing the best that God has for us in days ahead. Yet it was in this atmosphere that he performed this powerful miracle.

3. He revealed the progression of faith that was necessary to overcome. He kept working with Martha, Mary, and His disciples to show them His character. He encouraged them to believe. *"If you will believe..."* He kept saying, *"You will see the glory of God."* Our faith level must be raised to a new dimension in the body of Christ to overcome what is ahead. Resurrection, life, and faith have a proportionate relationship which is necessary for us to understand if we are to overcome what is ahead in our future.

4. Hopelessness is turned to resurrection power. Martha and Mary had lost all hope of seeing their brother again. However, Jesus kept breaking the power of hopelessness and encouraging them in faith. We must be delivered from hope deferred now!

To resurrect means to bring to view, attention, or use again; to raise from the dead; the rising again to life. Why did John devote so much time to this particular miracle? Was the raising of a dead person the issue? What was the relationship of this particular display of power and the events that were to come? Jesus stated that Lazarus's sickness was not unto death, but "for the glory of God." This was a culminating event in Jesus' life that eventually led to His own death and to the ultimate defeat of the dark powers holding humanity. Jesus overcame and was resurrected, and in doing so defeated hopelessness in our lives.

5. Power produces relationship or brings division. This display of the power of God, caused individuals to choose to either begin to plot Jesus' death, or to shout "Hosanna" and usher Him in as King. The body of Christ is about to be realigned over the display of the power of God. Don't expect everyone to receive the power that will be displayed in the days ahead. The power of God is life to many, but death to others.

6. The shout of "Come forth!" created a recovery. This is a season of recovery in the body of Christ. Hear the Lord shouting over you, *"Come forth!"* This means to escape, break out, bring forth, draw to an end, lead out, to depart from a condemned situation. *"Come forth!"* Let this shout of the Lord rise in your midst and declare a recovery of what you have lost in the past season. Below is a list for you to proclaim this supernatural recovery in your life, along with Scripture for you to declare victory in these areas:

- ♦ Recover lost and broken relationships (Isa. 58:12).
- ♦ Recover your prophetic call (Ps. 105:19).

- ♦ Recover delayed promises (2 Cor. 1:20).
- ♦ Recover the spirit and gift of faith (Rom. 1:17, Ps. 23:3).
- ♦ Recover the miracle of healing (Jer. 30:17).
- ♦ Recover your spiritual stability (Mal. 3:10, Ps. 129:8).
- ♦ Recover your financial stability (1 Sam. 7:11-14, 2 Chr. 20:6).
- ♦ Recover joy (Neh. 8:10).
- ♦ Recover wasted years (Joel 2:25).
- ♦ Recover the lost sheep stolen from your pasture (1 Sam. 17:34-37, 30:20).
- ♦ Recover the blessings of God (Prov. 3:32, Deut. 28:1-4).
- ♦ Recover all (1 Sam. 30).

God is Able!

I awakened one morning with the following words flowing through my spirit: "God is able!" The Holy Spirit seemed to be beckoning me to pray for God's people. In my prayers I was to declare God's ability to make each one of us able to overcome. I saw that we were hearing the Lord, however, our hearing was not turning into the necessary faith to overcome. I asked the Lord what the problem was and He said the following:

"My People are to go from faith to faith. They are struggling in their going. They have weak faith. Their expectations and hope of Me performing future happenings that will produce favorable outcomes in their lives is being sidetracked by circumstances. These circumstances are keeping them from entering into MY creative power. This new vigor, and strength that I can release will catapult them into this next dimension. I am able. Lean not on your own abilities, for I can enable you."

Faith should be growing and steadfast. Faith should be abiding and continuing. Faith should be producing work in God's

Kingdom. I see that we have grown anxious in the cares of this world. We have fallen into fear of failure, fear of harm, fear of abandonment, and fear of the future. We have forgotten God's ability to bless. *God is able to make you endure until you reach your "there"*! One meaning of the word endure is to repair a broken foot so you can step forward, continue on your journey, and possess the promise God has for you.

Receive His superabundant grace so that every hindrance in your path that is blocking you from reaching your "there" will be overcome and your life cycle will be fulfilled.

I declare anything that has caused your feet and spiritual walk to have broken peace, will be mended and you will continue on your journey to prophetic fulfillment. "And God is able to make all grace abound toward you, that you, always having all sufficiency in all things, may have an abundance for every good work" (2 Cor. 9:8). Receive His superabundant grace so that every hindrance in your path that is blocking you from reaching your "there" will be overcome and your life cycle will be fulfilled.

The United States in Days of War

We want to conclude this book by turning our focus on the prophetic fulfillment of our nation. September 11, 2001 was a defining day for the world. We stood in horror as we watched the World Trade Center crumble before our eyes as a result of the terrorist attacks upon America. Simultaneously, the Pentagon—the very

symbol of our military power, withstood great damage at the hands
of these extremists.

How do we respond to such an experience? Do we allow the
Spirit of God to lead us into intercessory prayer that will produce
change and determine whether we turn toward God or away from
God? Or do we allow fear and the sorrow of this loss to lead us into
bitterness, anger, revenge, and even greater defilements (see Heb.
12:15)? Do we cry out for mercy and grasp God's goodness in a
way we have never grasped Him before? Or do we have the reac-
tion that Job's wife had toward Job's sorrow and just say, "Curse
God and die."

Was it Judgment?

Was this a judgment on America? In an email sent out shortly after
the attacks, Dutch Sheets wrote: "Great caution should be exer-
cised in using the word 'judgment' to *define* these events. Many
Christians understand that America has been experiencing a degree
of judgment for some time – sin has wages (see Rom. 6:23). But
most biblical judgment is the inevitable, built-in consequence of
sin, not the direct hand of God. He didn't pronounce curses after
Adam and Eve's fall because He was an angry God who loves to
curse sinners. He did so because of the inherent results of their
actions. And He did it while covering their nakedness and promising redemption, a redemption involving great sacrificial love on
His part – the incarnation and death of His Son (see Gen. 3:15).
Also, rather than the direct hand of God, judgments are often simply the result of forfeiting God's favor and protection. Jonah 2:8
tells us: 'Those who cling to worthless idols forfeit the grace that
could be theirs.' A careful and compassionate explanation of reap-
ing, or the consequences of sin and of turning from God, should be
our definition of the events. I would advise not even using the term

'judgment' because the world will probably not hear anything else we say."

Rick Ridings from Israel sent the following interpretation of this event: "I believe the Scriptures show that such events are not specific judgment upon the individuals who happened to be in harm's way at that time. However, that does not take away from the fact that they can be judgment upon a nation and its idols. Jesus made this teaching clear in Luke 13:4,5: 'Or those eighteen who died when the tower in Siloam fell on them – do you think they were more guilty than all the others living in Jerusalem? I tell you, no! But unless you repent, you too will all perish.'

"I believe judgment comes upon cities and nations when the accumulation of our sins finally force a patient God to remove from us His gracious hand of protection, so that we get what we deserved all along. This principle is seen clearly, for example, in Isaiah 5:5: 'Now I will tell you what I am going to do to my vineyard: I will take away its hedge, and it will be destroyed; I will break down its wall, and it will be trampled. I will make it a wasteland, neither pruned nor cultivated, and briers and thorns will grow there. I will command the clouds not to rain on it.' The vineyard of the LORD Almighty is the house of Israel, and the men of Judah are the garden of his delight. And he looked for justice, but saw bloodshed; for righteousness, but heard cries of distress."

He goes on to say, "Totally aside from the question of whether this was some form of national judgment, is the question of present judgment and the shaking of demonic powers. I believe God is saying that judgment has begun on the twin pillars of the worship of Mammon and the worship of Allah. These two systems of false worship hold much of the world back from true worship to the true God, the God of Abraham, Isaac, and Jacob, and His only begotten Son and our Savior and Lord, Jesus Christ (Yeshua ha Mashiach)."

("How Should We Pray in the Aftermath of September 11th ?"
From Rick Ridings in Jerusalem, October 19, 2001)

Is the Best Yet Ahead?

Rebecca and I write much about lawlessness, terrorism, and anti-Semitism in the book *The Future War of the Church*. All three of these forces are rising in the earth realm. We are seeing a war over God's covenant with the earth. "The earth is the Lord's and the fullness thereof" (Ps. 24:1). The enemy knows that the Lord's fullness of purpose will be done in the earth realm. Therefore, there is a visible war raging that is backed by Satan's kingdom. This war is to stop the fullness of God's purpose manifesting in His people.

With this war now visibly raging, *is the best ahead*? With fundamental Islam becoming a global threat vying for the conversion and allegiance of souls in the earth, *is the best ahead*? With hate groups increasing, and hate breeding hate, *is the best ahead*? With the spirit of lawlessness manifesting in the next generation, *is the best ahead?* With wars and rumors of wars, *is the best ahead*? Psalm 20 is a wonderful confession to make:

"May the LORD answer you in the day of trouble; may the name of the God of Jacob defend you; may He send you help from the sanctuary, and strengthen you out of Zion; may He remember all your offerings, and accept your burnt sacrifice. Selah. May He grant you according to your heart's desire, and fulfill all your purpose. We will rejoice in your salvation, and in the name of our God we will set up our banners! May the LORD fulfill all your petitions. Now I know that the LORD saves His anointed; He will answer him from His holy heaven with the saving strength of His right hand. Some trust in chariots, and some in horses; but we will remember the name of the LORD our God. They have bowed down and fallen; but we have risen and stand upright. Save, LORD! May the King answer us when we call."

A Prayer Focus for America and the Body of Christ

Here are 10 prayer points to help focus us in days ahead:

1. Pray for God's power to be displayed in the earth realm. We are entering into a transition of power.

2. Pray for the restoration of the war mantle to the body of Christ. One of the greatest hindrances to prophetic fulfillment is for us to grow passive and stale in a time of war.

3. Pray for a supernatural repositioning of the body. This will allow us to stand in our proper boundaries.

4. Pray for a supernatural linking and binding between the generations.

5. Pray that the plowman shall overtake the reaper. This will move us from harvest to harvest. Amos 9, especially verse 13, is a key passage.

6. Pray that teams of plowmen will be connected together. No one is strong enough to plow alone. This is a time for apostolic, prophetic teams to rise up throughout the world.

7. Pray that humility abounds in the body of Christ. There will be many "humility meetings" in days ahead. These will be opportunities to restore covenants the enemy has attempted to break in the past.

8. Pray that the church will continue to increase in mercy toward the Jews. This will cause the world to resist the church. Watch for this to occur in cities with large Jewish populations (New York City, Miami, Los Angeles, Detroit, Houston, Buenos Aires, Paris, Moscow, etc.). Additionally, ministry to other ethnicities will also increase. Look for the wall of ethnicity to

break down. The church has not fully understood covenant but this will produce a restoration of God's covenant in the earth realm.

9. Pray for pastors. Expect God to do a new thing in the pastoral office. The shepherds will be very surprised by God. He will re-do pastoral thinking and cause the shepherds to be hungry for the glory. As God reorders the body of Christ, first apostles, second prophets, the pastor/teacher office will have to realign with God's purposes today.

10. Pray for confidence. Confidence results in boldness which results in awakening. The ability to produce the next move of God is within you. Do not keep looking at the past patterns of revival. Know the next move of God is already within you. This is a new move, like nothing we've ever seen before.

Is the best ahead? Yes, if His People who are called by His name will humble themselves and seek His face!

A Prophecy and Call to Advance!

God is saying to us, *This is a new day! Plant your feet and determine not to go backward. The enemy will assault you to press you backwards. Have I not said, "Without a prophetic vision the people perish and go backwards?" I am ready to revisit areas that have advanced My purposes but retreated at the day of battle. This is the beginning of the shaking of governments. There must be a confrontation of governments. My government on Earth is arising and causing entire regions to shake. I am restoring and raising up leaders. I am causing My governments and My gifts to align. This is creating great shakings from region to region throughout this land. This alignment is creating a shift in civil government.*

Today is a day of breaking off that which caused My church to retreat from the visitations of the past. Many advanced and then retreated! Now is a time to advance! There will be great connections occurring in My body in this advance. This will be the beginning of confronting sorceries, astrology, and witchcraft which have produced control. I am sending you forth and releasing supernatural wisdom. This wisdom will dethrone the sorcerers, astrologers, and practitioners of witchcraft throughout regions.

Love and confidence is arising in My body. From worship you will now move into a new supernatural dimension. Do not fear this call to the supernatural. The Pharaoh systems of this nation will begin to strengthen to keep My kingdom paradigms from forming and advancing in the earth! Do not fear these systems, but keep confronting through prayer the powers that have attached themselves to the structures of governments in your region. I will make you into a supernatural people who can rise up and overthrow that which has controlled you in the past and will control you in the future. My people are becoming a new, sharp threshing instrument. This threshing is producing shaking. This shaking is releasing Harvest. This is the beginning of a consuming fire. Fire must be in your heart. The fear of the supernatural is to be removed from you. Religious spirits and occultism has produced fear over the supernatural spirits. Therefore, they have retreated in their prayer life and fallen into passivity.

This is the beginning of a new day. Plant your feet. The window of opportunity for change is short and sweet. This will be a time that night watches are re-formed in your region, and I will revisit you in the night watch. I will visit my Bride as I described in Song of Solomon and knock upon her door. This is not a time for hesitation. Night watches will spring forth across this land. Once again these watches will open the door to Me, and I will come again. Therefore, I am calling watchmen to arise and cry out day and night for my Bride to be positioned near the door of opportunity in the nations of the Earth. Be positioned, ready to open the door of opportunity in your nation. My Bride must not hesitate to open the door. Harvest is waiting to come through the door into the storehouse of my Kingdom.

My will has been activated on Earth. I am advancing. Advance with Me. I will lead you into warfare. Many have grown fearful of confronting the enemy. I came to destroy the works of the enemy. I confronted both legalism and liberalism. I say rise up in worship that you might confront. Without confrontation, your enemy, the legalist, will gain much strength against you and narrow the boundaries of your freedom. If you will align yourselves properly and allow your gift to work within My government, I will guide you like a troop into warfare and make you victorious. Worship is arising. From worship, you will war! For a sound of war is coming into the heart of my people. Do not go backwards. Take off the old garments that would hinder you. My advance is now in the Earth.

*You have been blinded from the supply of the future. A new seer anointing is about to arise in My people. What you couldn't see in the past, you will now see. You've tried to connect and align with some, but now I will release a new anointing for connecting. You will see strategies of supply that have been hidden from you by occult powers. The seer anointing is coming back into your region. My people's eyes are about to see their supply. Advance is now in the Earth. Open your eyes and advance with Me. You will know Me as Jehovah Jireh! You will know Me as Jehovah Nissi! I, Lord Sabaoth, will now begin to release a manifestation from region to region throughout this land! Let Me clothe you with **favor** and **authority**! Advance!*

Subject Index